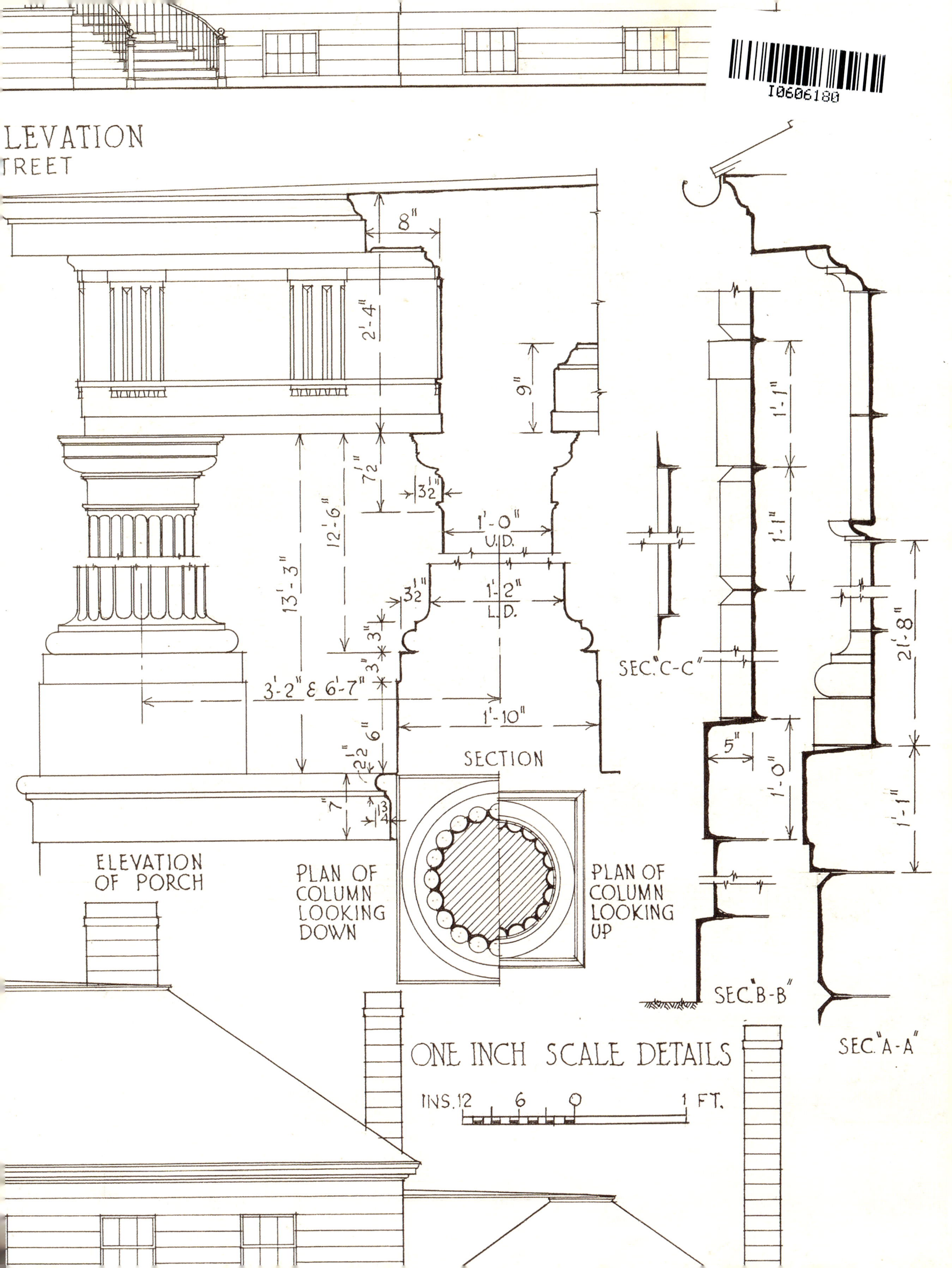

I0606180
LEVATION
TREET
ELEVATION
OF PORCH
SECTION
PLAN OF
COLUMN
LOOKING
DOWN
PLAN OF
COLUMN
LOOKING
UP
SEC."C-C"
SEC."B-B"
SEC."A-A"
ONE INCH SCALE DETAILS
INS. 12 6 0 1 FT.

GOVERNMENT HOUSE
HALIFAX

BY THE SAME AUTHOR

The Order of Canada: Genesis of an Honours System

Fifty Years Honouring Canadians:
The Order of Canada, 1967–2017

The Canadian Honours System, 2nd Edition

Savoir Faire, Savoir Vivre: Rideau Club, 1865–2015

Commemorative Medals of The Queen's Reign in Canada, 1952–2012

Canadian Symbols of Authority:
Maces, Chains, and Rods of Office

The Beginner's Guide to Canadian Honours

The Maple Leaf and the White Cross:
A History of St. John Ambulance and the Most Venerable
Order of the Hospital of St. John of Jerusalem in Canada

On Her Majesty's Service:
Royal Honours and Recognition in Canada

GOVERNMENT HOUSE HALIFAX

A PLACE OF HISTORY AND GATHERING

FOREWORD BY HIS ROYAL HIGHNESS THE PRINCE OF WALES

BELOW: *Grand Staircase*

CLARENCE HOUSE

For more than two centuries, Government House Halifax has served as a home for the Crown's representative in Nova Scotia. The oldest official residence in Canada, the building has been witness to many events significant in the life and development of the province, and Canada as a whole.

Described as "grey and graceful," Government House is a place where the Sovereign, their representatives and members of the Royal Family have come to greet Indigenous leaders, dignitaries, diplomats and members of the public since long before Canadian Confederation.

Constructed of materials sourced from throughout Nova Scotia and the Commonwealth, furnished and decorated with items from around the world, much of the story of Nova Scotia and Canada's growth over the past two-hundred years can be told through this living residence.

As one of the most significant surviving examples of Georgian architecture in Canada, I was pleased to see that the restoration of the building did much to preserve this living piece of built heritage, while making it accessible and more environmentally sound.

Beyond serving as a home away from home for members of the Royal Family and as a permanent abode for the Lieutenant Governor and their family, Government House has evolved to become the ceremonial home of all Nova Scotians. Therefore, during a recent visit to Canada in 2014, I was particularly delighted to be sworn into the Queen's Privy Council for Canada in the Drawing Room.

I am glad that this book helps to recount the history of the building, its many occupants and countless visitors, thereby preserving and sharing an important part of Canada's rich heritage.

AUTHOR'S NOTE

In the writing of this work the author, by the terms of his commission, was given full access to all relevant documents extant in the possession of the Government of Nova Scotia, and those documents related to the Government House Halifax held by the Provincial Archives of Nova Scotia and by Library and Archives Canada. The facts used by him have been verified from official sources, but he was left free to select and arrange the material. The inferences drawn and opinions expressed are those of the author himself.

VERSO: *Government House Garden Party, 1964*

ACKNOWLEDGEMENTS

THIS PROJECT, which has been going on sporadically for the last ten years, began shortly after my appointment as private secretary to the lieutenant governor. It has invariably been placed into abeyance on account of various official duties and other undertakings. The first person to encourage the development of a pictorial history of Government House was the Honourable Mayann Francis, ONS, who took up residence in Government House following the most substantial renovation that the building had undergone since the cornerstone was ceremoniously laid on 11 September 1800. Her persistent inquiries and support throughout the writing of this book have been much appreciated and valued.

I am most grateful to His Royal Highness The Prince of Wales for providing a foreword to this work. His Royal Highness has resided at Government House most recently during the 2014 Royal Tour, an occasion which included HRH being sworn into the Queen's Privy Council for Canada in the Drawing Room. His passion for heritage, architecture and the environment — both built and natural — is an inspiration.

A number of other former lieutenant governors and their families encouraged the development of this book, notably the Honourable Alan R. Abraham, CM, ONS, CD; the Honourable Myra Freeman, CM, ONS, MSM, CD; Brigadier-General the Honourable J.J. Grant, CM, CMM, ONS, CD, and Mrs. Joan Grant; Commander Richard Oland, CD, RCN; and Peter Moreira. Their intimate knowledge of the house and memories of life in the noble Georgian structure helped to add much texture to the story of Government House, its residents, staff, visitors and place in the history of Nova Scotia and Canada. Former vice-regal consort Gerda Hnatysnyn, CC, who herself authored a book on Rideau Hall, was also a source of encouragement and friendship.

A diverse array of friends, who have played a role in my previous works, were instrumental in aiding me with this particular project. Former honorary aide-de-camp Lieutenant-Commander Ian McKee, CD, RCN, who served for more than twenty-five years at Government House, provided many interesting anecdotes. My friends Commander Scott Nelson, MVO, CD, RCN, and Lieutenant-Colonel Carl Gauthier, MMM, CD, AdeC, were constant in their support, editorial comments and ideas in relation to this book. When the 2006–09 restoration of Government House concluded it was these two friends who traipsed around the 30,000-square-foot building, hammers in hand, and helped hang art and place furniture. Bruce Patterson, who has survived editing more than a million of my published words, is thanked for his perseverance and efforts to improve this text.

Colleagues within the government of Nova Scotia, notably Michael Laffin, former Manager of Operations at Province House, Scott Burke in the Speaker's Office and the staff at the Nova Scotia Archives were always free with their time and advice. My predecessors, Sheila Folk, who served as private secretary from 1974 to 1979, and Mary McGrath, who served in the same role from 1989 to 2000, were helpful with photos and memories of their time at Government House. My vice-regal private secretary colleagues, past and present, many of whom manage Government Houses across Canada, were similarly supportive and have taken a regular interest in this project.

Richard Jenkins, LVO, descendant of Sir Malachy Bowes Daly, is thanked for his interest and provision of photos from his ancestor during his tenure in Halifax. There is a symbolic symmetry to the fact we first met at Windsor Castle during a reception, with Her Majesty The Queen only a few metres away. I am appreciative of the perspective provided by the 8th Countess Carnarvon on running a large estate and for helping the author to better understand the very direct connection between the grand English country homes such as Highclere Castle and the Government Houses that serve as centres of official entertaining around the Commonwealth.

Fellow historian and co-conspirator on so many military-related commemorations and ceremonies, Colonel John Boileau, CD, assisted in directing me towards different avenues of research and for the last five years has been immensely supportive of my work. Dr. Dianne O'Neill of the Art Gallery of Nova Scotia is thanked for her assistance in relation to the elements related to artwork contained in this book. Indeed, the selection and placement of many of the finest pieces of artwork on display in Government House are on account of Dianne's keen eye. Dr. Martin Hubley was most helpful with a number of images. G. Brenton Haliburton, known for his expertise and work on the life of Lady Sherbrooke, was similarly supportive and helpful. At the Sir John Soane's Museum in London, Dr. Frances Sands was exceedingly helpful with some of the architectural aspects of this work. Blair Beed, a noted historian of Halifax, was generous with his time and explanation of various matters related to the development of downtown Halifax.

The Right Reverend Ralph Spence encouraged this work along the lines of the seminal works completed by his late friend Dr. Robert Hubbard, OC. Indeed, Hubbard was the first to undertake a comprehensive history of the provincial Government Houses with his work *Ample Mansions*. His sterling example has been a beacon of inspiration throughout the long journey to this project hitting the presses.

I am grateful to the Government of the Province of Nova Scotia for the opportunity to undertake this project and for the many different types of support that they have offered to me since I moved to this province in 2009.

Others who assisted with various aspects of this project include David McDonald, Legislative Librarian; Christopher Sullivan, Deputy Official Secretary to the Governor of New South Wales; John MacLeod from the Nova Scotia Archives; René Villeneuve from the

National Gallery of Canada and Kathleen Plow, daughter of Major General E.C. Plow, CBE, DSO, CD.

The household staff whom I have had the privilege to work with over the last ten years have always been helpful and interested in my work, especially as it relates to Government House, and the importance of this cannot be overstated. In particular Craig Walkington, MSM, CD, Communications Advisor to the lieutenant governor, has been a great support throughout my most recent work on this project. This richly illustrated book would not have been possible without the photographic talents of the Government House photographer, Michael Creagen, who has spent much of the last thirty years photographing events in and around the building. Jan Sykora is commended for his superlative arrangement of a book containing so many images. I owe thanks to the present residents of Government House, Their Honours the Honourable Arthur LeBlanc, ONS, QC and Mrs. Patsy LeBlanc, for their support and interest in my extracurricular work, and this project in particular.

My partner Matthew Malone, himself an architect, whom I met for the first time at Government House, has now survived six book projects and is owed a great deal of credit. His tolerance for my work ethic and peculiarities when it comes to "bashing out another book on the laptop" are appreciated beyond any written credit. Finally, my late mother Dr. Sharon McCreery is gratefully acknowledged. Her love of antiques and the delight she found in watching Government House come together with every new donation and auction find, remain fond memories.

Christopher McCreery, MVO
Government House
HALIFAX

VERSO: *Ballroom Entrance*

BELOW: *Her Majesty Queen Elizabeth II and Grand Chief Ben Sylliboy, 2010*

INTRODUCTION

Grey and Graceful: A Place of Gathering & Hospitality

THE OLDEST OFFICIAL RESIDENCE in Canada, Government House Halifax sits upon the traditional territory of the Mi'kmaq people. Through the Treaty of Peace and Friendship 1725 and subsequent treaties, the connection between the Mi'kmaq people and the Crown was formalized and remains a foundational aspect of modern Canada. The kinship and connection endures through the special relationship that exists between The Queen of Canada and the Mi'kmaq people. The home of the Crown in Nova Scotia has a special role in fostering this bond as a place where the Queen's representative and Mi'kmaq leaders have gathered to affirm this relationship and to build upon it.

Government House is the home of the Sovereign's representative in the province, the ceremonial home of all Nova Scotians and a place of gathering and hospitality. It has also served as a home away from home for members of the Royal Family over its two century history. As a living residence, it continues to function with much of the same purpose it had when Sir John

and Lady Wentworth took up residence within its walls in late 1805. As the role of the lieutenant governor has expanded beyond its constitutional responsibilities to encompass the promotion of the province and its people, so too has Government House come to welcome an increasing number of guests and visitors.

Unlike many other official residences, the history of Government House Halifax is woven deeply into

ABOVE: *Government House, December 2014*

BELOW: *View from the rear garden*

national, provincial and municipal history. We should not forget that when the cornerstone was laid on 11 September 1800, the lieutenant governor discharged a number of what are now largely distinct roles as the King's representative, commander-in-chief, premier, head of the civil service and mayor. Government House has many facets: it serves as the home for the lieutenant governor, the administrative office of the lieutenant governor, a place where official government business is transacted, Commonwealth and foreign diplomats are welcomed, citizens are recognized with honours of the Crown and other awards and where

BELOW: *Government House, 1952*

numerous volunteer organizations are welcomed and commended for their good works.

This illustrated history of Government House tells the story of not only the building and the Crown collection, but also of its many residents, the household staff and the historic — and occasionally amusing — events which have transpired within the walls. Many signal moments in the history of Nova Scotia and Canada have taken place within Government House. The swearing-in and meeting of the first cabinet following the attainment of Responsible Government, debates surrounding Nova Scotia's inclusion in Confederation, the appointment of the first French Canadian as governor general of Canada by The Queen herself, the swearing-in of The Prince of Wales into the Queen's Privy Council for Canada, the granting of an official pardon to the late Grand Chief Gabriel Sylliboy and centennial commemorations surrounding the 25th and 85th Battalions Canadian Infantry and their gallant service in the First World War. On an individual level, countless new Canadians have taken their Citizenship Oath in the Ballroom, thereby joining the Canadian family. Over two centuries, thousands of proud families have come to Government House to witness the presentation of gallantry decorations such as the Victoria Cross and Military Cross, while others have come to be presented with the insignia of the Order of the British Empire, Order of Canada, Order of Nova Scotia and a myriad of jubilee and long service medals — even the Governor General's Literary Award. These proverbial signposts in

ABOVE: *Drawing Room entrance*

BELOW: *Engraving of the Government House Gardens, 1889*

our collective history have occurred within the elegant "grey and graceful"[1] walls of the Georgian gubernatorial mansion in downtown Halifax.

Various articles and booklets have been written about Government House, notably Sir Adams George Archibald's *Government House at Halifax,* published during the closing year of his tenure as the Queen's representative in Nova Scotia — which, it will be remembered, followed his rather remarkable earlier service as a Father of Confederation and the first lieutenant governor of Manitoba. In 1939, J.S. Martell wrote and published *The Romance of Government House,* which was subsequently updated in four editions and seven printings, the most recent being released in 1990. These important earlier works should not be forgotten as they helped to preserve elements of the building's history and character that would have otherwise been lost.

It is also worth noting the significant contribution made by other historians of Canada's official residences, notably Dr. Robert Hubbard, OC, who penned two works on Rideau Hall, and another, *Ample Mansions: The Vice Regal Residences of the Canadian Provinces,* and Gerda Hnatyshyn, CC, who wrote *Rideau Hall: Canada's Living Heritage,* the work that this publication is broadly based upon.

The present work is the first lengthy publication to examine the history of Government House Halifax in a multifaceted manner. The thematic structure has been contrived to take the reader through the early history of Government House, then on to the various functions fulfilled by the building, a chapter on the various Royal residents, the state rooms as they are presently set up and then on to chapters about the Crown Collection and symbols of the Office of the Lieutenant Governor in Nova Scotia. Throughout the book various vignettes have been included, touching upon assorted lieutenant governors, their consorts and some members of the household staff.

INSET: *Lieutenant Governor Mayann Francis and multifaith leaders following blessing ceremony*

From September 2006 until November 2009 the building was, for the first time in its history, unoccupied for an extended period of time. For three years an extensive restoration and renovation was undertaken by a dedicated team of architects, engineers, project managers, electricians, plumbers and craftspeople. This talented group ensured not only that the building once again became habitable and functional, but that it would also become accessible and open; transformed into a ceremonial home, continuously at the ready to welcome dignitaries and visitors alike. Just over $6.25 million dollars were invested into bringing the oldest official residence in Canada back to life.

We can glean much about the growth and evolution of Canadian society through the lens of Government House as a social setting, political cauldron and gathering place for those in high office and the broader citizenry. This place, which was once largely open only to those at the pinnacle of society, has gradually been transformed into a home of the people — well beyond the annual New Year's Day levée where members of the public were welcomed into Government House to greet the Governor

REOPENING 2009

FOLLOWING THE THREE-YEAR extensive restoration and renovation of Government House undertaken by a dedicated team from the provincial Department of Transportation and Infrastructure Renewal, the keys to the building were turned over to the Private Secretary on the afternoon of 12 October. The house returned largely to its original layout; the paint and finishes restored to Georgian period colours; the electrical, mechanical, heating, plumbing and information technology systems all completely replaced and modernized; and the following month was consumed with placing furniture, unpacking silver, china and crystal and installing art.

On 4 December 2009, following with the tradition set when the cornerstone of Government House was laid in 1800, a special blessing ceremony was held. Lieutenant Governor Mayann Francis presided over a Mi'kmaq smudging which opened the 8:30 am event, and this was followed by prayers and readings offered throughout Government House by ten different religious leaders from various Christian denominations and the Jewish, Hindu and Muslim faiths.

Six days later on 10 December, Lieutenant Governor Mayann Francis; the Minister of Transportation and Infrastructure Renewal, Bill Estabrooks; the Commander of Maritime Forces Atlantic, Rear-Admiral Paul Maddison; the Commander of Land Forces Atlantic Area, Brigadier-General David Neasmith and a colour party from the Royal Canadian Navy held an inaugural flag raising at Government House. With the lieutenant governor about to formally take up residence in the building, the vice-regal flag, along with the national and provincial flags and the Royal Union flag, were raised for the first time in more than three years on the property. Government House once again returned to being a functional vice-regal residence.

ABOVE: *Lieutenant Governor Clarence Gosse during the 1978 New Year's Day Levée*

MIDDLE: *Lieutenant Governor Arthur LeBlanc during the 2018 New Year's Day Levée*

BELOW: *Team which restored Government House between 2006–09*

on the opening of a New Year, or to present compliments, complaints or petitions. One of the first petitions to be presented to the lieutenant governor after the attainment of Responsible Government came in February 1849 when Chief Pelencea Paul and nine other Chiefs brought their petition to Government House and then took it to members of the Legislature at Province House.[2]

Throughout this work the term "governor" and "lieutenant governor" are used interchangeably, as has long been the practice in Nova Scotia. Although the position of governor of Nova Scotia was downgraded to lieutenant governor in 1784 as a result of administrative changes made to Britain's North American colonies, the practice of referring to the Sovereign's representative in the province as the "governor" or the "guv" has continued into the present day. No doubt, Sir John Wentworth, who had been the last Royal Governor of New Hampshire, did not discourage this practice, nor have his successors. Nova Scotians seem attached to the idea that, as the cradle of Representative, and then Responsible, Government in Canada, their chief executive has a historical claim to retain the old designation which dates back to the earliest days of Acadia.

ABOVE: *Royal Tour Invitation and Admittance Card, 2010*

BELOW: *Royal Tour Staff Pass and Staff Security Pin, 2010*

In the presence of
Her Majesty The Queen
and
His Royal Highness The Duke of Edinburgh

Her Honour the Honourable Mayann E. Francis
Lieutenant Governor of Nova Scotia

has the honour to invite

A. Bruce McDonald, MC

to a ceremony rededicating Government House
Monday, June 28, 2010 at 4:30pm

R.S.V.P. BY JUNE 18
(902) 424-7019
LGOFFICE@GOV.NS.CA

Government House
1451 Barrington Street, Halifax, Nova Scotia

DRESS:
BUSINESS SUIT
AFTERNOON DRESS

ENCLOSED ADMITTANCE CARD MUST BE PRESENTED WITH VALID PHOTO IDENTIFICATION

No. 387

Government House Rededication Ceremony

ADMITTANCE CARD

Monday, June 28, 2010 at 4:30pm
Government House
1451 Barrington Street, Halifax, Nova Scotia

THIS CARD MUST BE PRESENTED AT THE GATES OF GOVERNMENT HOUSE WITH VALID PHOTO IDENTIFICATION

10

VERSO: *Government House Winnipeg, residence of the Lieutenant Governor of Manitoba*

BELOW: *The Queen departing Government House Halifax, 30 June 2010*

ONE

An Enduring Tradition: Government Houses Around the Commonwealth

THE TERM GOVERNMENT HOUSE is an unusually descriptive moniker for any edifice. It indicates a place where the activities of government are transacted and also that the building is a home, for both the state and its senior-most officeholder. The very expression is a metonym for the residence of the head of state or their representative and also the household and office which supports them in the discharge of their duties. Throughout the Commonwealth, the term has come to be closely intertwined with the role of the Crown and its various representatives: the governors general, governors, lieutenant governors and administrators. Even in those countries which have adopted republican forms of government, with a president in place of a sovereign, Government Houses remain — retaining their original designation or occasionally restyled as State House. Just as every country has a head of state, each head of state has at least one official residence, a place for official functions and government business to take place, but also to serve as a place to live for the person at the apex of the state.

Government Houses are places where both the executive and ceremonial functions of the state transpire with consistency. In Nova Scotia, prior to the attainment of Responsible Government in 1848, Government House was the locus of all major decisions taken by the governor of the province and his executive council (the Cabinet). As Canada's parliamentary democracy evolved and was refined, the law-making role was transferred to the legislature; nevertheless, elements of the executive function continue to be carried out at Government

BELOW: *Rideau Hall, 1953*

RECTO: *Rashtrapati Bhavan, residence of the President of India, formerly the residence of the Governor General of India*

House. Of course, the lieutenant governor today no longer proposes laws or policies; these decisions are made on the advice of the elected government, which, although appointed by the Crown, is the representative of the citizenry.

Like the role of the Crown in Canada's constitutional monarchy, Government House is a place where the ceremonial and legal/constitutional functions of the province converge. The ceremonial and symbolic duties of the Sovereign and their representatives are defined as being the *dignified* role of the Crown, while the legal and constitutional functions are defined as the *efficient* role of the Crown, which are now largely exercised by elected politicians. The British newspaperman Walter Bagehot first explained this distinction in his 1867 work *The English Constitution*. While Government House is a residence and place of hospitality, it is also a locus of authority and the Crown's symbolic home in the province.

The grandest of all the Government Houses is *Rashtrapati Bhavan*, in New Delhi, India. At 200,000 square feet, it is the largest official residence in the world, larger even than the Palace at Versailles. Designed by Sir Edward Lutyens, it was originally the home of the Viceroy of British India, and later the governor general of India following independence in 1947. Today *Rashtrapati Bhavan* is home of the President of India, continuing to function as other Government Houses do around the globe — albeit on a grander scale at the epicentre of the world's largest democracy.

The French had a long tradition of providing quarters for their overseas officials. In the Canadian context, most notably the governor's quarters at the Fortress of Louisburg and the palatial Chateau Saint Louis in Quebec City. Nevertheless, the general concept behind a Government House is taken directly from the English country estate. Government Houses in Canada, past or present, were never intended to be replicas of Buckingham Palace. It was impractical to transplant such a building into North America, certainly not at public expense.

Most of the early governors who served in British North America were members of the British aristocracy. They were men of means and possessed a city house in London and one or several country estates — thus setting up a Government House was an extension of this tradition. Without any substantial metropolitan centres there was no 'city house' for the governor to reside in. Yet there was ample land and space upon which to build a country estate and it is from this tradition that Government Houses were established in early Canada.

BEYOND BRICKS & MORTAR

It is natural to ask why an official residence is of any importance at all, especially when one considers that in Canada only a few public office holders other than the governor general, eight of the lieutenant governors, prime minister, leader of the opposition in the House of Commons and speaker of the House of Commons enjoy such a benefit. These buildings serve not only as a place of official entertainment and hospitality, they serve as an outward symbol of the state's presence and authority

BELOW: *Government House Halifax, 1890*

— the Crown's majesty revealed in bricks and mortar in the Canadian context. Heads of government, ministers, diplomats and guests are summoned to meet with the governor to be sworn in, deliberate, be celebrated and be recognized with honours and awards. Government Houses also serve as a place of political neutrality, unlike the legislature where the partisan deliberations and machinations unfold quite naturally as part of the political environment. In other jurisdictions, not just throughout the Commonwealth, the heads of state and their representatives almost invariably have a place outside the legislature where they are able to discharge their constitutional and ceremonial duties. Government Houses in Canada have also become places to showcase the art, culture and heritage of each jurisdiction, living museums and places where important moments in the life of the province have taken place and continue to transpire. Canada's Government Houses, like those in Australia, are among the world's most accessible official residences where the public is welcomed for events, performances and tours, in addition to the formal governmental and diplomatic activities undertaken by the various vice-regals.

The closure of Government Houses is something that has occurred in a number of Canadian provinces and in a number of Australian states as well. From time to time — invariably during a period of fiscal restraint — debate over the cost of maintaining an official residence and the required household staff has been brought up in the press and legislature. When an official residence is closed, it strikes against the Crown's symbolic presence, results in a reduction of prestige and the status of the governor, eroding the dignity of the office in a tangible manner. No longer are citizens summoned to attend events at Government House; rather, they trundle off to a rented venue, usually devoid of history or presence. There is also an associated symbolic imbalance created, in that the removal of a Government House often leaves the premier with a more impressive office in the legislature than the lieutenant governor.

The various attempts to close Government House Halifax have been related to the expense of maintaining the physical building, and not due to any animus towards the Crown or lieutenant governor personally. With the achievement of Confederation the province was relieved of covering the cost of the lieutenant governor's salary but not the cost of Government House. While some government buildings were transferred from the provinces to the federal government, notably lighthouses, post offices, canals, railway lands and armouries, others remained the responsibility of the province. The Fathers of Confederation felt that while the salary of the lieutenant governor should be covered by the Dominion government — given the vice-regal holder is a federal officer — the cost of the various Government Houses, other than Rideau Hall in Ottawa, should remain the responsibility of each province. This

BELOW: *Parliament of Canada, Ottawa, 1867*

was outlined in section 108 of the *Constitution Act, 1867*. By December 1873, official word came from Ottawa that "'Government House Block' and the 'Governor's Stable' and 'Garden Lot' … are not required for the use of the Dominion of Canada … it is hereby ordered that the said properties shall be, and they are hereby appropriated for the use of the Legislature and Government of the Province of Nova Scotia."[3]

By the late 1880s Nova Scotia, like all of Atlantic Canada, was in the grips of a recession and during the 1888 budget debate the recently elected MLA for Queen's County, Albert Hemeon, introduced a resolution to effect the "sale or lease of Government House, and there lands attached thereto."[4] Hemeon was incensed that since Confederation the province had spent not less than $80,392.81 on the maintenance of the building. While there was discussion of selling the property, one idea was to see it converted into a hotel. The resolution was adjourned, Premier William Fielding being unimpressed with the proposal. It was next the social-democratic Cooperative Commonwealth Federation in 1948 which called for Government House to be "converted into a museum or art gallery … and that a more modest residence … be provided for the chief executive."[5] This would be the last legislative attempt to relieve the citizens of Nova Scotia of Government House. The situation in other provinces has been quite different. In total, five Government Houses have suffered closure; although three of these have subsequently re-opened, only one has returned as an official residence.

With the construction of the Parliament buildings in Ottawa it was originally planned that a new Government House would be built to replace the cobbled together structure that became Rideau Hall, residence of the governor general in the Dominion capital. "Having widely overspent on the Parliament Buildings project,

ABOVE: *Government House Fredericton, closed 1890–1999*

BELOW: *Government House Sydney, Australia, Sydney Opera House is in the background*

ABOVE: *Chorley Park, Government House Toronto 1915–1937*

BELOW: *Razing of Chorley Park, 1961*

the government preferred to enlarge and refurbish Rideau Hall in 1865–66.[6]

In 1890, New Brunswick's Government House in Fredericton was closed largely as a result of the aforementioned regional recession. The lieutenant governor's residence and office was removed to a more modest building until 1999, when the lieutenant governor returned to Old Government House, Fredericton. During the 1937 provincial election, Ontario's Premier Mitchell Hepburn announced his intention to close the palatial Government House Chorley Park in Toronto. Although the closure would not take place until 1938 following an extended and exceedingly complex dispute and a series of negotiations between Hepburn and Prime Minister Mackenzie King.[7] In an act of architectural vandalism, Chorley

INSET: *Charred beam*

Park was razed in 1961, the only official residence in Canada to be purposefully destroyed. Alberta's bombastic Premier William Aberhart would follow Hepburn's lead and not only announce but proceeded with the closure of Government House Edmonton in 1937. Saskatchewan was next to follow the cascade of closing vice-regal residences in 1944 when Premier Tommy Douglas closed Government House Regina and the lieutenant governor moved his office into the Hotel Saskatchewan in Regina.

The premiers of these three provinces made no secret of their desire to close their Government Houses for reasons of economy, although this was only really true in the case of Saskatchewan. Hepburn's motivations, though complex, can be boiled down to a running battle with his political nemesis William Lyon Mackenzie

FIRE!

ONE OF THE GREATEST ENEMIES of Government Houses has always been fire. Five Canadian Government Houses have been consumed by fire, and Government House Halifax, at the direction of Sir John Wentworth, was constructed specifically to withstand such a catastrophe.

On Sunday morning, 20 August 1854, while most of Halifax was at church, fire broke out in the high attic. "It took the whole fire force of the city three hours to put the flames out, and then the entire centre roof and several apartments below were destroyed. The wings escaped."[8] The slate roof of the building had suffered leakage issues since the Wentworths moved in, and by coincidence, 21 August was the last day for builders to submit tenders for replacing the original slate roof! For two months the Lieutenant Governor, Sir John Harvey, and his wife moved into the Belvedere, the private residence of Colonel John Bazalgette, aide-de-camp to a number of previous lieutenant governors and also onetime administrator of the province. Repairs to the fire-damaged roof were expanded to include replacement of the chimneys and drainage gutters; the entire project was completed by the end of October 1854 at a cost of £5,000, and the lieutenant governor resumed residence shortly thereafter.[9] In his first Speech from the Throne following the repairs Sir John noted:

> You will be gratified, I am sure, to learn that I have resumed the occupation of Government House, seriously injured by the late fire, but renovated and refurbished in a style that bespeaks your munificence, whilst demands my grateful acknowledgements.[10]

A later fire on the second floor broke out at 10:30 am on Monday 18 April 1864 and caused damage, mainly to furniture and the walls; however, this was contained relatively quickly. A more minor fire occurred in 1904; however, this is only revealed as the result of a bill included in the public accounts of that year.

ABOVE: *Government House Regina, closed 1944–84*

BELOW: *Bois du Coulonge, Government House Quebec City, formerly residence of the Governor General of British North America and then of the Lieutenant Governor of Quebec, 1867–1966*

King. Alberta's Aberhart was also seeking retribution against Lieutenant Governor John Bowen for refusing Royal Assent to three unconstitutional bills passed by the Alberta Legislature. Bowen was essentially evicted from Government House, there being a reduction in the size of the staff, provision of electricity and telephone services. Quebec's Government House, Bois-du-Coulonge (formerly Spencerwood) burned in 1966 and would be replaced by a parochial suburban residence which was closed in 1997. The closure and sale of the post-1966 Quebec residence was taken by the separatist Parti Québécois, which had no desire to be seen as supporting the Crown or the federal appointee who resided there. Saskatchewan would return Government House to official vice-regal use in 1984, after an extended period as a veterans' hospital and then as an adult education centre. Alberta's Government House in Edmonton has never been returned to its former glory; although the lieutenant governor occasionally holds events there, its primary use is as the provincial government conference centre.

VERSO: *The Habitation at Port Royal*

TWO

Sir John Wentworth's Dream

SINCE THE CAPITAL OF NOVA SCOTIA was moved from Annapolis Royal to Halifax in 1749, the city has known three Government Houses. The earlier period, which began in 1603, saw the arrival of the French and their first contact with the Mi'kmaq, without whose aid there would have almost certainly been no Acadia or permanent European settlement in the area for many years. With the establishment of the Habitation at Port Royal in 1605, the Crown's representative, the Governor, took up residence in the modest quarters afforded him within the walls of the fort. As the military and administrative centre, Port Royal became the principal settlement, locus of authority and capital of Acadia. The Habitation would be destroyed during the Battle of Port Royal in October 1613, in which the English besieged the town and colony. Thus, began more than a century of conflict between French and English, with the people of Acadia and Mi'kmaq often caught between the two great powers who were vying for international ascendency.

While many of the Governors lived within the walls of the fort, a number would rent houses in the town of Port Royal, notably François-Marie Perrot in 1684.[11] Most of the buildings in the town had thatched roofs and were quite modest. In 1702, construction was commenced on a new fort, which makes up the present Fort Anne. A residence for the Governor was included in the plans for the fort, along with a barracks and other military structures.[12] Following the fall of the town to the British in 1710, it was renamed Annapolis Royal in honour of Queen Anne.

The French were not the only people who settled at Port Royal. In 1621 King James VI of Scotland granted Sir William Alexander, Earl of Stirling, all of the territory which today makes up Nova Scotia and New Brunswick. The first Scottish settlers arrived at the present-day site of Annapolis Royal and established Charles Fort. While there was no formal governor of New Scotland, Sir William Alexander was made Hereditary Lieutenant General of Nova Scotia. However, there was no official residence. The initial presence of Scottish settlers concluded in 1632 after the Treaty of Saint-Germain-en-Laye was signed between Britain

VERSO: *Lord William Campbell*

BELOW: *The second Government House*

on which small pieces of ordinance were mounted for its defence."[16] The frame, cladding and windows for the building were brought via boat from Boston, there being no cut lumber suitable for building. Completed in the fall of 1749, a short three months after the arrival of the British, Governor Cornwallis would hold the first meeting of the Governor's Council on 14 October 1749 in the Government House Dining Room at a large oak table which had been taken off HMS *Sphinx*. Although unpretentious, this Government House would serve as the centre of government, place of official hospitality and residence for the Governor, if only temporarily. In 1755 this building was removed from the site to make way for a more substantial structure. Finished building materials being scarce, the first Government House was sold and pulled by horses down to the corner of George Street and Bedford Row. The building was relocated again in 1775, this time to "the beach and placed at the corner of the street leading to the steam boat landing"[17] where it remained until 1832, when it was razed.

THE SECOND GOVERNMENT HOUSE

The second Government House was constructed in 1755, on the very same site of the first Government House, it being the centre of the growing town of Halifax. With its advantageous view of the harbour and defensible location, it remained the ideal place for the centre of government. It was during the tenure of Governor Charles Lawrence that a new two-and-a-half storey clapboard structure was erected. Lord William Campbell's time as Governor, from 1766 to 1773, saw the construction of a "ball room at one end, and several other improvements were made to the building. ... It was surrounded by a terrace neatly sodded and ornamented.

BELOW: *Prince William Henry (the future King William IV)*

The building was of wood, two and a half stories high."[18] A lively engraving of this building was rendered by Richard Shortt in 1761, depicting the building painted to appear as stone, accompanied by a number of outbuildings, surrounded by a fence and sentry boxes. John Parr, who served as Governor from 1782 to 1783 and as Lieutenant Governor (the post was reduced in rank in 1784) from 1786 to 1791, was rather fond of his official residence and emoluments associated with serving as the King's representative in the province:

> I have found everything here to exceed my expectations, have met with the greatest civility from all Ranks of People, a most excellent house and Garden, a small farm close to the Town ... plenty of Provisions of all sorts except Flower [sic], with a very good French Cook to dress them, a Cellar well stock'd with Port, Claret, Madeira, Rum, Brandy, Bowood Strong Beer &c ... plenty of Coals and Wood against the severity of Winter, a house well furnish'd and warm Cloths, that upon the whole my Dear Grey, your friend Parr is a happy and comfortably seated, as you could wish an old friend to be.[19]

The house was of a substantial size when one considers it was able to accommodate almost sixty people for official entertainment, as described by the diarist William Dyott, who served in Halifax as a young Lieutenant and would later rise to the rank of General in the British Army. During the Royal Visit of Prince William Henry (the future King William IV), Dyott recorded some of the official frivolity:

> In the evening at a ball at the Governor's. We went about seven; his Royal Highness came about half after, and almost immediately began country dances with Miss Parr, the Governor's daughter. We changed partners every dance; he danced with all the pretty women in the room, and was just as affable as any other man. He did me the honour to talk a great deal to me before supper during the dance. We went to supper about twelve, a most elegant thing, nearly sixty people sat down ... After supper he gave five or six bumper toasts ... We had a most jolly evening, and we retired about two o'clock.[20]

Upon arriving in Halifax in 1792, following his appointment as lieutenant governor of the province, Sir John Wentworth took up residence in the second Government House. With the passage of time he developed an unfavourable assessment of the building. Wentworth eventually wrote to the Colonial Secretary,

BELOW: *Benning Wentworth*

the Duke of Portland, complaining that the house had been built "chiefly of green wood … and the larger timbers generally rotten."[21] It would be several years before Wentworth began his campaign to have a grander Government House constructed — what would become the third, and current, Government House. By 1806 this, the second Government House was partially deconstructed and sold to Mr. John Trider, Sr., who used the remnants in the "construction of a building on the road leading to the tower at the head of Inglis Street, formerly owned by Colonel Bazelgette, and afterwards the residence of Mr. George Whidden."[22] The building was later converted into a home for infants and unwed mothers and this later burned in 1898.[23]

THE THIRD GOVERNMENT HOUSE

To better understand the reasons why the third, and present Government House, was located, designed and constructed as it was, we must consider the building's first residents, Lieutenant Governor Sir John Wentworth and his wife, Lady Frances "Fanny" Wentworth. In many ways, Government House Halifax might just as well be known as 'Wentworth Hall,' given the leading role that Wentworth played in securing funds and land to construct the Georgian mansion. Wentworth suffered attacks levied at him by members of the House of Assembly due to cost overruns but was nevertheless determined to see the building completed in the style of an English country estate. As we shall see, the Wentworths had already lost their palatial summer residence in New Hampshire on account of their loyalty to the Crown, and the vice-regal couple were determined to finally reside in a Georgian mansion befitting Sir John's station and the rising importance of their new province in the British Empire.

As the grandson of John Wentworth the elder, who served as lieutenant governor of New Hampshire from 1717 to 1730, and the nephew of Benning Wentworth who served as the first Royal Governor of that province from 1741 to 1766, Sir John grew up in affluent surroundings and was accustomed to the best.[24] The Wentworth family home at 346 Pleasant Street in Portsmouth was erected in 1763 for local merchant Henry Appleton, and in 1764 it was purchased for £4,000 by Sir John's father, Mark Hunking Wentworth. Overlooking what was then known as Smith Pond (subsequently renamed Lake Wentworth), the imposing two-and-a-half storey wooden clapboard Georgian mansion with a hip roof and three chimneys[25] served as the ersatz Government House for New Hampshire following Sir John's appointment in 1766 as the second — and last — Royal Governor, a post

ABOVE: *Government House, Portsmouth, New Hampshire*

BELOW: *Wentworth-Woodhouse*

he would retain until fleeing the American Revolution as a Loyalist refugee in 1775. Throughout Britain's American colonial possessions, it was the practice for Governors to reside in their personal residences, which served as Government Houses for the duration of their appointment — only in a few of the 13 American Colonies was there a purpose-built Government House. Sir John rented the Pleasant Street home from his brother-in-law for £67 a year, a cost borne by the New Hampshire Legislature.

Wentworth critically described this residence in Portsmouth as a "small hut with little comfortable apartments."[26] Wentworth's father had a more generous assessment of the home: "On the one side we look over the town and down the river to the boundless Atlantic Ocean; on the other side we overlook a place for a garden, bounded or rather separated from the fields by a large sea-water pond, which enlivens the rural scene." One gains an idea of Sir John Wentworth's perception of size when one considers the reality displayed in a photo of the same building which depicts a substantial elegant multi-storey home festooned with tall windows.

Along with his town residence, Sir John had constructed a summer home on Lake Winnipesaukee, 80 km outside of Portsmouth, near Wolfeboro, New Hampshire, in 1769. When Wentworth House was completed it was said to be the largest home in the province and sat upon 4,300 acres, and on which Sir John spent £20,000 of his personal fortune to build.[27] The building burned in 1820 and, unfortunately, no drawings or plans remain of the imposing structure. Archaeological evidence shows that the building was 104 feet in width and 42 feet deep.

It is not difficult to trace where Sir John's sense of grandness for an official residence came from. Wentworth had long been a friend of the second Marquess of Rockingham, Charles Watson-Wentworth. Wentworth spent a great deal of time at Rockingham's country estate, Wentworth-Woodhouse.[28] At 250,000 square feet it remains the largest private residence in the United Kingdom, and is more than 8 times the size of Government House Halifax.

It was from the Wentworth family home on Pleasant Street in Portsmouth that Sir John and Lady Francis fled the American Revolution aboard HMS *Scarborough*, after Sir John executed his last official act as Governor, proroguing the New Hampshire legislature. The Wentworths first travelled to Boston and then on to New York, where Sir John was active in aiding the Loyalist cause — but it was to no avail. Realizing that the fight for his homeland had been lost, he requested permission to sail to England and would ultimately be granted leave to depart British North America, arriving in England in April 1778.

On their journey to England the Wentworths spent a short period in Halifax and then made their way to London. Having lost their various properties, possessions and much of their wealth, the Wentworths prevailed upon relatives and friends for assistance, and Sir John began the search for a new post and sought compensation for his considerable losses.

One might ask why the very well-connected Wentworths did not seek to remain in England following their exile from New Hampshire. While England may have been their metaphorical home and "the mother country," it is certain that they were more at home in colonial society — especially being at the pinnacle of all that was going on. In London they were just another Loyalist couple in search of purpose, and without a

SIR JOHN WENTWORTH, BT (1737–1820)

THE GOVERNOR who we have to thank for the construction of Government House Halifax, Wentworth was a long-serving and occasionally controversial figure — in large part due to his role in the building of Government House. A close relative of two Governors of New Hampshire, Wentworth was born into a wealthy and influential American colonial family. He studied at Harvard University, receiving his BA in 1755 and MA in 1758. Despite a rather comfortable upbringing, he was very much at home in the wilderness and somewhat of an expert on trees. By 1766, he was appointed Royal Governor of New Hampshire and Surveyor General of the King's Wood for all British North America, succeeding his uncle Benning Wentworth. He served as Governor of New Hampshire until 1775 when the events of the American Revolution forced him and his wife, Lady Francis Wentworth, to flee on account of their loyalty to the Crown and Britain.

Wentworth arrived in Nova Scotia in 1783 and was appointed as Surveyor General of the King's Wood and became responsible for overseeing the harvesting and preservation of arbour resources to aid the Royal Navy. King George III appointed Wentworth lieutenant governor of Nova Scotia in 1792, a post he would hold until 1808. In this role, Wentworth oversaw the reconciliation of the province's finances and an improving economic outlook for Nova Scotia. Although a highly experienced governor, Wentworth was not always on cordial terms with his legislature, and nowhere did this become more apparent than in his dealings with the elected body in relation to expenditures on the new Government House.

He and his wife were known for their lavish parties, high living and various liaisons — having what was in essence an open marriage. Wentworth also oversaw an ambitious, yet ultimately unsuccessful, plan to resettle Maroons (descendants of Jamaican slaves) in the province — the cost of which, combined with expenditures on Government House, played a part in tarnishing his otherwise distinguished legacy. In 1808, after 16 years as the King's representative in Nova Scotia and more than a quarter century serving in vice-regal office, Wentworth's appointment came to an end. He would die in Bedford in 1820 and is interred in the crypt of St. Paul's Anglican Church.

BELOW: *King George III*

peerage, land or significant wealth, they were not part of the elite. Following the American Revolution, "London had little need for the services of colonial customs officials, judges, councillors, or landowners."[29] This group included former Royal governors, of whom there were nearly two dozen residing in London by the late 1780s. There was the additional fact that Sir John, as the Surveyor of the King's Wood, had much better financial prospects in British North America than he ever had in England.

Having served the Crown with distinction and loyalty during a most tumultuous period, he naturally felt it his due that some great appointment would be conferred upon him by King George III. This was an important time not only for the Wentworth's quest for new purpose and fortune, but also for the building that would become Government House. Given the social circles in which the Wentworths travelled, they were eminently familiar with a number of great English country homes and the estates of the peerage and landed gentry in and around London. It is from the designs and decoration of some of those truly palatial and opulent country houses built during the Georgian period, that we find many of the elements that would come to be incorporated into Government House Halifax.

By late 1791 Sir John had at last obtained a new appointment and on 24 January 1792, the *London Gazette* announced "The King has been pleased to constitute and appoint John Wentworth, Esq; to be His Majesty's Lieutenant-Governor of the Province of Nova Scotia, in the Room of John Parr, Esq; deceased."[30] The Wentworths then made their way home to North America, and to Nova Scotia, a somewhat less well-developed province than Sir John's native New Hampshire. Given his previous experience as a Royal Governor, Wentworth was "a man very specially prepared for the job of governor of N.S."[31] Wentworth went to some effort to study his new province's

"needs, and promoted legislation to meet with the same intelligence and tact which had characterized his administration in New Hampshire ... there were the construction of good roads, the encouragement of education, and the maintenance of military preparedness."[32]

For the first few years that Sir John resided in Government House, he seemed content with the building; however, we should not forget his fastidious approach to residences. The assembly voted £380 for repairs to Government House in 1793, but this appears to be mainly to address deferred maintenance. It is worthwhile speculating that Wentworth, a seasoned governor, did not express his desire for a grander Government House shortly after arriving due to the pressure of administering a vast array of matters in relation to governing the province. Being politically astute and having learned a few things as the result of his direct experience with the American Revolution, he sought to study the personalities and partisan

BELOW: London Gazette *entry announcing appointment of John Wentworth as Lieutenant Governor*

Numb. 13381. [37]

The London Gazette.

Published by Authority.

From Saturday January 21, to Tuesday January 24, 1792.

Whitehall, January 24.

THE King has been pleased to constitute and appoint John Wentworth, Esq; to be His Majesty's Lieutenant-Governor of the Province of Nova Scotia, in the Room of John Parr, Esq; deceased.

LENT Preachers appointed to preach before His Majesty, for the Year 1792.

Feb.	22	Ash Wednesday,	Dean of the Chapel, Lord Bishop of London.
	24	Friday,	Dean of Canterbury, Dr. Buller.
	26	Sunday,	Lord Bishop of Durham.
	29	Wednesday,	Dr. De Salis.
March	2	Friday,	Dean of Christ Church, Dr. Jackson.
	4	Sunday,	Lord Bishop of Lincoln.
	7	Wednesday,	Mr. Tattersal.
	9	Friday,	Dean of Winchester, Dr. Ogle.
	11	Sunday,	Lord Bishop of Salisbury.
	14	Wednesday,	Mr. Haggit.
	16	Friday,	Dean of Lincoln, Sir Richard Kaye.
	18	Sunday,	Lord Bishop of Chester.
	21	Wednesday,	Mr. Gretton.
	23	Friday,	Dean of Carlisle, Mr. Milner.
	25	Sunday,	Lord Bishop of Carlisle.
	28	Wednesday,	Dr. Cooke.
	30	Friday,	Dean of Peterborough, Mr. Sutton.
April	1	Palm Sunday,	Lord Archbishop of Canterbury, or Lord Archbishop of York.
	4	Wednesday,	Mr. Gape.
	6	Good Friday,	Dean of Westminster, Lord Bishop of Rochester.
	8	Easter Day,	Lord Almoner.

SALISBURY.

LENT Preachers appointed to preach at His Majesty's Chapel at Whitehall, on Wednesdays and Fridays, for the Year 1792.

Feb.	22	Ash Wednesday	Dean of Norwich, Dr. Turner.
	24	Friday	Dr. Price.
	29	Wednesday	Mr. Powys.
March	2	Friday	Dr. Fisher.
	7	Wednesday	Mr. Kynaston.
	9	Friday	Dr. Glasse.
	14	Wednesday	Mr. Keysall.
	16	Friday	Dr. Parker.
	21	Wednesday	Mr. Taylor.
	23	Friday	Dr. Nicol.
	28	Wednesday	Mr. Butt.
	30	Friday	Dr. Langford.
April	4	Wednesday	Mr. Longe.
	6	Good Friday	Dean of Chichester, Mr. Miller.

SALISBURY.

War-Office, January 24.

15th Regiment of Foot, Henry Roberts, Gent. to be Ensign, by Purchase, vice Edward Letherland, promoted.

33d Regiment of Foot, Lieutenant Evan Mac Pherson, from the Half-Pay of the late 82d Regiment, to be Lieutenant, vice Robert Molesworth, replaced on Half-Pay.

36th Regiment of Foot, Ensign George Horne, from the Half-Pay of Waller's late Corps of Foot, to be Ensign, vice Robert Cockburn, who exchanges.

37th Regiment of Foot, Ensign George Mackenzie, from the Half-Pay of the 71st Foot, to be Ensign, vice John Kennedy, who exchanges.

50th Regiment of Foot, John Campbell Morrison, Gent. to be Ensign, by Purchase, vice Hudson Lowe, promoted.

60th Regiment of Foot, Francis G. de Montmollin, Gent. to be Ensign, by Purchase, vice William Thomas, promoted.

64th

[Price Eight-pence.]

landscape which he had been commissioned to oversee and administer. There was the additional fact that Nova Scotia was awash in debt and there was scarcely enough revenue to cover salaries to run the province, let alone embark upon unprecedented public works schemes.

Wentworth's first recorded complaints about his abode and office commenced in 1797, and to emphasize that the building was not suitable, Wentworth relocated himself to his lodge located on the Bedford Basin ten kilometres outside of town, and which took forty minutes to travel to and from.[33] The Governor was not totally isolated from the capital given the operation of a signal telegraph, which could call him into town with five minutes notice. The same year that Wentworth raised his concerns about the official residence with Lord Sydney, the Colonial Secretary, and a number of local politicians, the provincial Legislature passed an act authorizing the construction of a Legislature and a Government House. Up to this point deliberations of the Legislature had been taking place in a number of meeting halls and even taverns. Ten years earlier, in 1787, the Legislature passed an act authorizing the sale of Crown lands within the

BELOW: *Provincial Act authorizing the construction of a new Government House*

408 C. IX. Anno tricesimo nono Georgii III. 1799

Raiſing money for the building a market-houſe: rents, &c. to go to its repair.

III. *And be it further enacted,* That it ſhall and may be lawful for the Grand Jury of the ſaid county, from time to time, to raiſe, by preſentment, in the uſual form, ſo much money as may be neceſſary to build, repair and erect, the ſaid market-houſe; and the rent of the ſtalls, and ſtandings, in ſaid market, together with all fines and forfeitures ariſing in purſuance of this Act, ſhall be applied to the keeping of ſaid market-houſe in repair, and to no other uſe.

CAP. IX.

An ACT in amendment of an Act, paſſed in the Thirty-ſeventh year of His Majeſty's reign, entitled, An Act for appointing Commiſſioners to determine upon a proper ſituation in the Town of Halifax, and to purchaſe Lots of Ground, if neceſſary, to erect a Public Building for the accommodation of the General Aſſembly, Court of Chancery, Supreme Court, and Court of Admiralty, and Public Offices, and for procuring Plans and Eſtimates for a Building hereafter to be erected for the reſidence of the Governor, Lieutenant-Governor, or Commander in Chief for the time being.

Preamble.

WHEREAS *by the aforeſaid Act it is provided, that there ſhall be erected a range of Public Buildings, for the ſittings of the General Aſſembly, and Courts of Juſtice, and for the Public Offices, and alſo a Government-Houſe, for accommodation of a Governor, Lieutenant-Governor, or Commander in Chief, and by the ſaid Act it is intended, that the ſaid range of Public Buildings ſhall be firſt erected: and whereas the preſent Government-Houſe is in ſo ruinous a condition, as to be unfit for the reſidence of the Governor, or Commander in Chief of this Province, whereby it becomes more immediately neceſſary, to proceed to the erection of a houſe ſuitable for his reception and accommodation:*

The erection of Public Buildings for ſitting of General Aſſembly, &c. to be deferred and a houſe for the accommodation of the Governor built.

I. *Be it therefore enacted, by the Lieutenant-Governor, Council and Aſſembly,* That the erecting of the range of public buildings, for the ſittings of the General Aſſembly and Courts of Juſtice, and of the Public Offices, be deferred, and that inſtead thereof, a ſuitable houſe be erected, with proper offices, and conveniences, on the lot of ground purchaſed for the ſaid range of public buildings, or on the ground which may be purchaſed contiguous thereto, for the accommodation of the Governor, Lieutenant-Governor, or Commander in Chief of this Province, which houſe, when erected, ſhall be called the Government-Houſe of the Province of Nova-Scotia, and ſhall be appropriated for the reſidence of the Governor, Lieutenant-Governor, or Commander in Chief of the Province of Nova-Scotia, for the time being; and to no other uſe and purpoſe whatſoever.

Governor to appoint Commiſſioners, to ſuperintend ſaid building

II. *And be it further enacted,* That it ſhall and may be lawful for the Governor, Lieutenant Governor, or Commander in Chief for the time being, to nominate and appoint other Commiſſioners, in the room and place of ſuch of the Commiſſioners nominated in the ſaid Act, whoſe offices have become, or ſhall hereafter become vacant, by death, reſignation or removal, and the perſons ſo appointed, together with thoſe appointed by the ſaid Act, and continuing in their office, ſhall be Commiſſioners for building the ſaid Government-Houſe.

Materials collected for Public Building to be uſed for Government-Houſe.

III. *And be it further enacted,* That it ſhall and may be lawful for the ſaid Commiſſioners to employ and uſe, in the building of the Government-Houſe hereby authoriſed to be erected, ſuch parts of the materials already contracted for, or purchaſed for, the intended range of public buildings, as they may find neceſſary, and to ſell and diſpoſe of ſuch other parts of the ſaid materials as may not be wanted for the ſaid Government-Houſe: and the monies, thence ariſing, ſhall be applied, by the ſaid Commiſſioners, to and for the uſes of the ſaid Government-Houſe.

IV.

1799 Anno triceſimo nono Georgii III. C. X. 409

Purchaſe of lot of ground, whereon to erect the government houſe of the Province of Nova-Scotia.

IV. *And be it further enacted,* That the ſaid Commiſſioners, or the major part of them, with the approbation of the Governor, Lieutenant-Governor, or Commander in Chief for the time being, may and ſhall determine upon, and purchaſe, ſuch and ſo many lots of ground in the town of Halifax, contiguous to the ſaid lot of ground lately purchaſed for the range of public buildings, as may be ſufficient and ſuitable whereon to erect a houſe for the accommodation of the Governor, Lieutenant-Governor, or Commander in Chief for the time being. *Provided always,* That the purchaſe money of ſuch lots do not exceed the ſum of one thouſand five hundred pounds. *And provided alſo,* That the whole expence of building, and fully completing the ſaid Government-Houſe within, and without, with all the ſuitable conveniences, ſhall not exceed the further ſum of five thouſand four hundred pounds.

Old government houſe to be appropriated to the ſittings of the General Aſſembly, Courts, &c.

V. *And be it further enacted,* That ſo ſoon as the ſaid Government Houſe ſhall be erected, and completed, fit for the reſidence of the Governor, Lieutenant-Governor, or Commander in Chief, and he ſhall have removed thither, the houſe and lot of ground now uſed and appropriated as the Government-Houſe, ſhall be uſed and appropriated for the ſitting of the General Aſſembly and the Courts of Juſtice, and ſuch Public Offices as it will accommodate, or which may be built, or provided, on the ſaid lot of ground.

general vicinity of Halifax to aid in the raising of funds to cover the erection of a legislature building as well as courts and public offices for members of the minute provincial public service. This earlier act made no reference to a new Government House being part of the buildings required for the growing province.

The 1787 act remained dormant until the financial position of the province had improved significantly — notably under Wentworth's guidance. With the improved economic situation, a new act was passed in 1797 in aid of the construction of a new suite of government buildings. The text of the act was unusual as it specifically referenced the loathsome condition of Government House — as though the insertion of such an observation into the preamble of an act would somehow quell public concern over the replacement of the governor's home:

> WHEREAS by the aforesaid Act it is provided, that there shall be erected a range of Public Offices, and also a Government House, for accommodation of a Governor, Lieutenant-Governor, or Commander in Chief, and by the said Act it is intended, that the said range of Public Buildings shall be first erected; and **whereas the present Government-House is in so ruinous a condition, as to be unfit for the residence of the Governor**, [bold added by author] or Commander in Chief of this Province, whereby it becomes more immediately necessary, to proceed to the erection of a house suitable for his reception and accommodation.[34]

While at first glance it would seem the requirement for a purpose-built legislature building should have taken precedence over the construction of a new Government House, having the governor residing outside the city, and the poor condition of the existing Government House, were viewed by Members of the Legislative Assembly to be problematic enough to warrant their allowing the Government House project to be given priority. There was also the fact that Government House was used on a near-daily basis for the transaction of official business, such as meetings of the Governor's Council, while the legislature tended to only be in session for 30–40 days per year.[35] There was also agreement that while the Legislature authorized £10,500 towards the Government House, Wentworth also approved £6,000 for roads and bridgeworks. The costs associated to building the new official residence would eventually become a major source of tension between the lieutenant governor and some members of the legislature.

One must consider why the Colonial Office, which was responsible for all matters related to British North America, did not discourage Wentworth from embarking upon such an ambitious project. The population of the province at the time was just cresting the 60,000 mark, and the annual government expenditures increased from £14,930 in 1797 to £26,208 in 1799, with revenue being drawn primarily from customs duties and the sale of Crown lands. Certainly the Colonial Office saw the value in the Crown and the Imperial Government's representative being housed in a suitable building where official business could take place. As with all significant public buildings, regardless of location, the purpose is not only to provide a place for governing to take place, but such structures also serve as tangible projections of the state's authority, majesty and permanence — veritable monuments not only to those in authority at a particular time, but to the enduring presence of government. Amongst the local population, especially the United Empire Loyalists, there was a desire to have an outward sign of the Crown's presence and permanence. For the Loyalist refugees who fled the American Revolution, the erection of such a majestic edifice was an affirmation of their success and loyalty, despite having faced great hardship and loss as a result of their devotion to Britain and the Crown. This was also a period when Britain's

BELOW: *Raj Bhavan, Kolkata, residence of the Governor of West Bengal, India, formerly Government House Calcutta*

international prestige had nearly fully rebounded from the losses of the American Revolution. Halifax was a growing military and economic centre, of vital importance to the Royal Navy and Britain's military position in British North America and the Atlantic. Simultaneous with the construction of Government House Halifax, the British commenced building Government House in Calcutta — today the *Raj Bhavan, Kolkata* and the residence of the Governor of West Bengal — in the then capital of British India. At nearly 84,000 square feet, three times the size of Government House Halifax, it cost £63,291.[36] Other imposing Government Houses would be built across Canada, India and Australia over the same period into the 1850s.

It being agreed by the Governor and members of the Legislature that a new Government House should be constructed, the practical matter of where the building should be situated, what it should look like and other logistical details had to be determined — and of course there would have to be a cornerstone-laying ceremony.

After the amended bill was passed, Wentworth granted Royal Assent and it became law. As it was also an appropriation bill, it was the custom for the Speaker to make a statement. Speaker Richard J. Uniacke, a man who played a key part in the development of Nova Scotia, the abolition of slavery and the emancipation of Roman Catholics in the province, noted:

> Fifty years have just elapsed since the first English settlers landed here. There are members of both His Majesty's Council and House of Assembly who can recollect when the first tree was felled on the spot where you now preside over the Legislature of a free and happy country. We should be the basest and most unworthy of all people were not our hearts filled with sentiments of the most grateful and affectionate attachment to our beloved Sovereign, who from the first day of his reign to present has never ceased to heap favours on this Province and constantly to consult the safety and happiness of his faithful people. The unparalleled favour of our just and good king, and influence of the great and powerful nation from which we derive our origin have, under Divine Providence, been the cause of our prosperity. This country, which but a few years ago was a dreary wildness, is now a flourishing Province, inhabited by a numerous happy, brave and loyal people. It shall be our duty to perpetuate these sentiments to the latest prosperity, thereby to secure the present connection between Great Britain and this country to the end of time. ... [w]e have not much to give, but what we have we give cheerfully and with pleasure. After seven years of rigid economy we are enabled to vote a considerable sum of money to erect a more suitable dwelling for the representative of His Majesty to reside in.[37]

There was an ebullient tone to Uniack's speech, and this was not without good reason. The financial position of the province had improved substantially under Wentworth's administration; Nova Scotia's economy was growing; and the eighteenth century was drawing to its conclusion with confidence that the new century would bring greater success, security and prosperity to Britain's leading North American colony.

BELOW: *Richard Uniacke*

LOCATION OF BUILDING SITE

The location of the new Government House was the source of considerable debate, not out of concern for the governor's new home being made too remote from the centre of town, but rather out of the fear on the part of some legislators that their new meeting house would be remote and inconvenient. In the 1797 act that called for the construction of a legislature and new Government House, it was decided that the legislature should be constructed across from the St. Paul's Churchyard (now the Old Burying Ground), the same site where Government House is located today. This location "was not acceptable to all members of the House,"[38] and after extended debate, the 1797 act was amended, noting that the proposed location was too remote. A committee was subsequently struck to decide where Government House should be located — some members of the Legislature clearly preferred the site of old Government House for the location of their new meeting house. The committee considered three potential locations for the governor's new residence; interestingly enough, none of them included the pre-existing site where Government House had stood since 1749. The options considered by the committee were:

1) Cochran lot with the addition of the School lot, and another owned by Mr. Grant (across from the Old Burying Ground);
2) The Gerrish estate (near the naval dockyard);
3) The Governor's South Farm (located in the Bedford Basin).

The Committee believed that acquiring title to the Grant lot would be difficult, and obtaining approval from the Imperial Government to acquire permission to build on the Governor's South Farm land would take too much time; therefore, it was decided that Government House should be constructed on the Gerrish estate. Shortly thereafter, concerns surrounding acquiring the Grant lot evaporated and it was decided to erect the new Government House on the Cochran, School and Grant lots, which were subsequently acquired for this purpose; this was the section of land located across from the Old Burying Ground, with the front of the building facing Hollis Street and the service entrance facing Pleasant Street.

There are several references to a building having been on the site where Government House now stands. "In 1750, a public hospital was erected, and was maintained by the government for several years. At about 1766, by request of the Magistrates, this hospital was granted for an alms house. The building stood at the northern part of the land now occupied by the Government House."[39]

VERSO: Government House view by Woolford

BELOW: Christ Church Shelburne, Shelburne, Nova Scotia

THREE

Building a Stately Georgian Home in the Wilderness

ALTHOUGH THE LEGISLATURE voted in favour of a new Government House being constructed, there remained many details to be worked out by the lieutenant governor, the commissioner of works and his board, the architect and even those who would eventually erect the stone edifice. Once the initial details were arranged, building designs, site plan and excavation could begin. This would be followed by a ceremonial cornerstone-laying ceremony for what was, up to that point, the largest house building project in Nova Scotia's history. The cornerstone laid true, Wentworth went on to jeopardize his relationship with the Legislature and taint his otherwise excellent reputation with fellow Nova Scotians in order to realize his dream of a stately official residence.

BUILDING SITE & PLAN & ARCHITECT

Before the construction of the new building could commence, quite aside from questions related to funding the project, the important matters of choosing an architect and devising a plan for layout and elevations had to be agreed upon. The architectural design of Government House was undertaken by Isaac Hildrith and was heavily influenced by the building's first resident, Sir John Wentworth. Hildrith was born in England in 1741, would immigrate to Virginia in 1770 and, after fighting against the rebels in the American Revolution, would eventually find his way to Shelburne, Nova Scotia. In the Loyalist stronghold, Hildrith oversaw the design and construction of Christ Church Shelburne, and this did much to establish his reputation. His first project in

ABOVE: *Rendering of the original front facade of Government House by Woolford, c. 1819*

BELOW: *Plan of the main floor of Government House by Woolford, c. 1819*

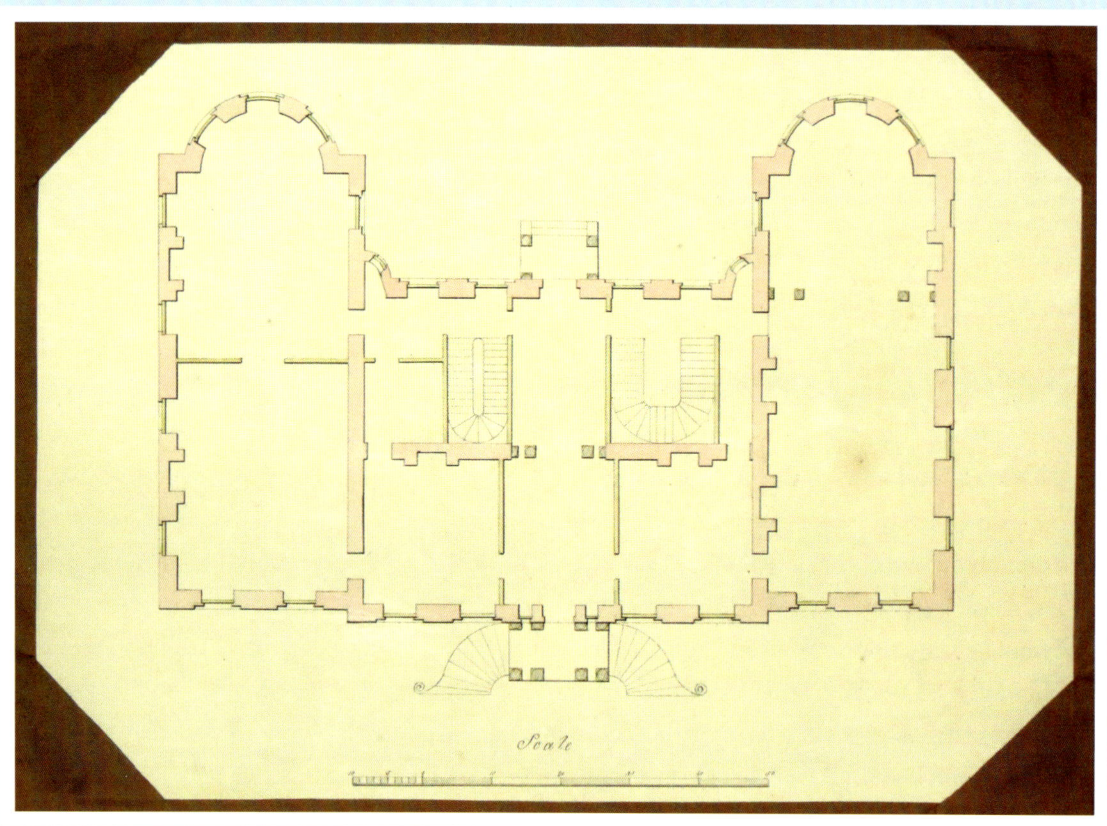

ABOVE: *Kedleston Hall*

MIDDLE: *Kenwood House*

BELOW: *Nostell Priory*

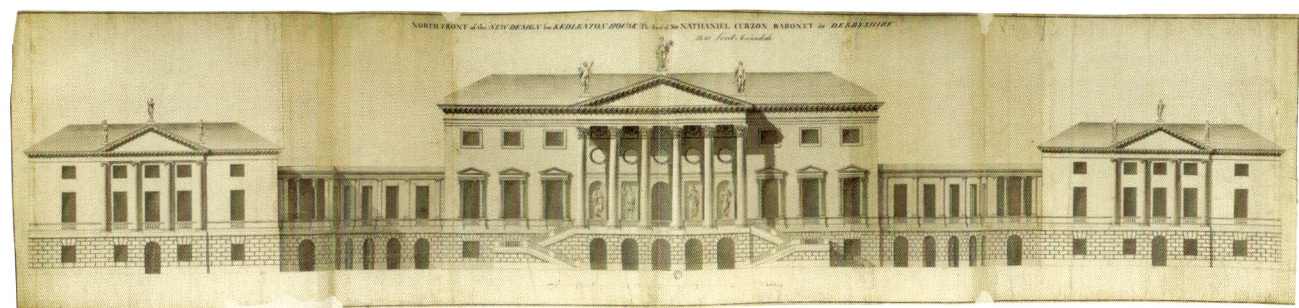

surmounted by the upper register articulated by pilasters, is also similar to Kenwood House's park fronting façade. The Hollis Street façade is strikingly similar to Nostell Priory and Kedleston Hall.[43] Sir John's role in the design of the building can most prominently be seen in the scale and size of the structure: at the time of its construction, it was the largest purpose-built Government House in British North America.

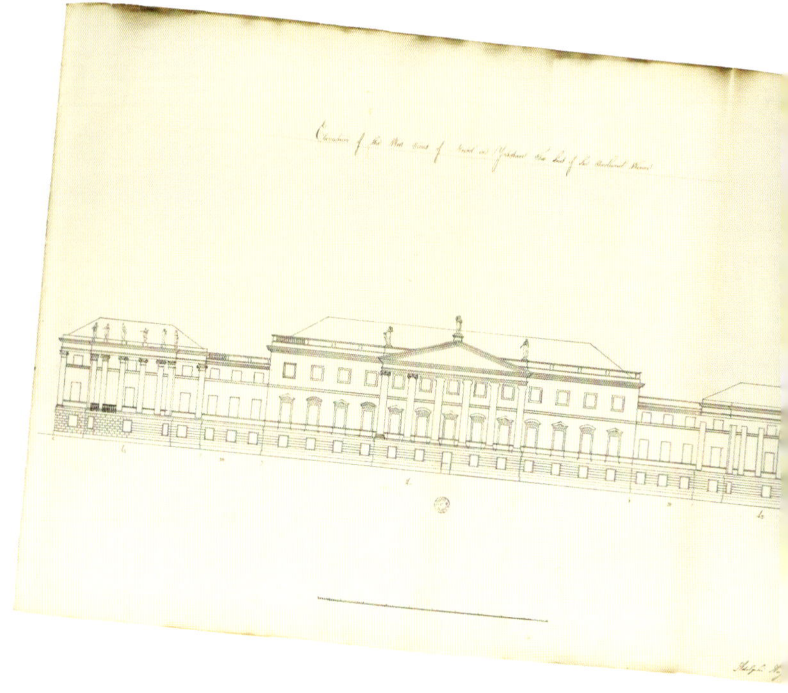

BRICKS, MORTAR, STONE, WOOD & SLATE

The decision to build the house out of stone and brick, and not wood, was one of the major reasons for the escalation in the cost of the project.[44] Through the 1790s, Halifax, which was composed almost entirely of wooden structures, suffered a number of disastrous fires. After a blaze tore through part of the Prince's Lodge, Wentworth received from a concerned friend some helpful correspondence related to the most effective methods for fireproofing a building. In his response Wentworth noted:

ABOVE: *Red brick interior wall of Government House*

BELOW: *Stone foundation*

> I am obliged in your friendly consideration of the losses and inconvenience occasioned by the late Fires. And have mentioned your ideas to the Commissioners of the building of the Govt. House — They are deterred by apprehensions of increased expense, but have built all the divisions of the Kitchen or lower Story with stone and lime eighteen inches thick, and the Floors are to be laid with flag or squared stone — the ceilings will be thick lime and plaster — the doors, window sashes and furniture only will be combustible, and cannot furnish fuel or communication to penetrate beyond any of those apartments, which may take fire. Care is also taken to have a water pipe in each room of these, and the floor over them capable of a great supply of water.[45]

In all likelihood this was the first such house in Canada to be equipped to suppress the outbreak of fire. In retrospect, it is also easy to surmise that the choice of such building materials is the principal reason why the structure has endured more than two centuries largely unscathed, this despite several fires and the Halifax Explosion. In negotiating the details of the new building, Wentworth ensured that the latest in fireproofing techniques were incorporated into the structure.

At significant expense, stone was brought in from Pictou, Antigonish and Cape Breton, while 'building stone' was imported from Lunenburg and Lockeport, with red flagstone from Antigonish and blue rubble stone and flat stone from the North West Arm of Halifax for the foundation walls. Red brick made in Dartmouth was used for much of the interior supporting walls. Some of the granite that faces the building is believed to have come from Aberdeen, Scotland, and arrived in Halifax as ballast in cargo ships. It is interesting to note that the Adam brothers also owned a granite quarry in Aberdeen that was

BELOW: *Government House view by Woolford*

ABOVE: *Drawing Room fireplace*

known for supplying paving slabs to London and places abroad where such durable material was required for the building of fortifications.[46]

The sandstone that covers the façade of Government House, along with that of Province House, was brought in from Wallace, Nova Scotia, and was originally known as 'Ramsheg.' The Provincial Treasurer, Michael Wallace, who oversaw the finances for the province's public works projects, insisted on the use of this stone given its availability and economical cost. His enthusiasm for use of the stone is, at least in part, responsible for his name being given to the town of Wallace, Nova Scotia, which had previously been known as Remsheg.[47] Sand was brought from Shelburne, Eastern Passage and McNamara's Island for use in the mortar and drainage beds. The roof was clad in Scottish slate, and lead from England was used to seal the hips of the roof and areas around the chimneys.

THE MAROONS

THE MAROONS WERE DESCENDANTS of African slaves who had originally been transported to Jamaica by the Spanish to work on sugar plantations. The Maroons came to Nova Scotia at the behest of Wentworth, following an uprising in Jamaica whereby the Maroons fought to maintain their freedom. In 1796 just over 1,000 Maroons arrived in Halifax. Some were employed in expanding the fortifications on Citadel Hill, while others would eventually be employed in the initial excavation work for the construction of Government House. Although the Maroons were paid on par with what white labourers earned, their situation in Nova Scotia was not a happy one as a result of racism, the harsh climate and lack of support from the government. By the fall of 1800 more than half of the Maroons sailed out of Halifax for Freetown, Sierra Leone.

Wentworth also had a personal if somewhat unconventional connection to the community, in that he had a Maroon mistress and she would bear him a child, George Wentworth Colley (1804–1893), some of whose descendants continue to live in Halifax.

The interior finishes included plaster walls and marble fireplace mantles, while white and yellow pine boards from Cornwallis Townships were used for the flooring along with red pine from Tatamoagouche and Annapolis. The finest mahogany was imported from Belize (what was at the time British Honduras) for a number of the interior doors on the main floor of Government House — although as a cost-saving measure, faux painted doors made to look like mahogany were also used.

THE BUILDERS

Under Isaac Hildrith's able direction, the construction of Government House commenced in the fall of 1799 with the laying out of the building's orientation and digging of the foundation. This initial work was undertaken by Maroons and soldiers of the British Army (fusilier miners) who were stationed in Nova Scotia.

The Chief Mason, John Henderson, was a Scot who oversaw the day-to-day work on the building site. We get a glimpse of the level of activity on the site from an 1801 invoice for labour which notes that over a six day period between 18 and 23 May, twenty-three men were working on site. Their wages ranged from a high of 7 shillings per day for the chief mason to 4 shilling 2 pence per day for the less skilled labourers. This six days of work cost the provincial treasury £28.12.1. Hildrith would be paid £75 for the preparation of the plans and building estimates, and after the project was completed, a joint committee of the legislature noted they had "full conviction of the ability and professional skill of Mr. Hildrith, and satisfactory proofs of his seal, integrity, and diligence in conducting the work he has been engaged in, respectfully recommend[ed], that, with his discharge, the Sum of Fifty Pounds, be granted him as a Testimonial of the public opinion of his Merit and Service."[48] It would be the first such award of recognition to any architect in Canada.

AN AUSPICIOUS START

The laying of the cornerstone was certainly the most ceremonious occasion in the province's history, and the event took place nearly a year after initial work on the site began. The entire occasion was recorded in the *Royal Gazette*:

> On Thursday last this long projected and necessary building was begun under the auspices of His Excellency Sir John Wentworth, Bart. On this pleasing occasion a procession was formed at the present Mansion House [old Government House] which preceded by a band of musicians playing 'God Save the King,' 'Rule Britannia,' and other appropriate airs, went to the site prepared for the erection of the edifice, where the corner stone was laid with customary forms and solemnities, and a parchment containing the following inscription was placed in a cavity cut for that purpose in the centre of the stone;
>
> DEO FAVENTE
>
> The corner stone of the Government House, erected at the expense of His Majesty's loyal and faithful subjects of Nova Scotia, pursuant to a grant of the Legislature of the Province, under the direction of Michael Wallace, William Cochran, Andrew Belcher, John Beckwith and Foster Hutchinson, Esquires, for the residence of His Majesty's Governor, Lieutenant Governor or person exercising the chief civil authority, was laid on September 11th, Anno Domini, 1800, in the 40th year of the reign of His Most Sacred Majesty, George the III.
>
> By His Excellency Sir John Wentworth, Baronet, LL.D., Lieutenant-Governor and Commander in Chief of His Majesty's Province of Nova Scotia and its dependencies; Surveyor-General of Woods in all

His Majesty's Territories in America, and Colonel of the Royal Nova Scotia Regiment;
Vice-Admiral Sir William Parker, Baronet, Commander in Chief of all His Majesty's Ships and Vessels employed, and to be employed, in North America;
Lieutenant-General Henry Bowyer, Commanding His Majesty's Forces in the Province of Nova Scotia and its Dependencies;
Colonel the Right Honourable John Lord Elphinstone, Commanding His Majesty's 26th Regiment of Foot, and
Colonel George Augustus Pollen, Member of British Parliament, Commanding His Majesty's Fencible Regiment of Loyal Surrey Rangers.
Accompanied by —
The Honourable Sampson Salter Blowers, Chief Justice of the Province

The Honourables, Henry Newton }
Alexander Brymer }
Thomas Cochran } Members of
Charles Morris } His Majesty's
John Haliburton } Council
Henry Duncan }
Benning Wentworth, and }
James Brenton }

Richard John Uniacke, Esqr, Speaker and member of the House of Assembly in town.
Robert Murray Esqr., J. Pellew, Esqr., Joseph Bingham, Esqr., R. Lawrie, Esqr., Henry Carew, Esqr., and J. Sykes, Esqr. Captains in the Royal Navy.
Lieutenant-Colonels Lagard, Wetherall, Burrows, Benton, Burroughs, Earles, Edwards and Hope.
Majors Walker, Torrens, Thesiger and Aldridge; Field Officers of His Majesty's Forces in Nova Scotia.
The Commissary General, the Deputy Judge Advocate

JOHN ELLIOTT WOOLFORD (1778–1866)

A NOTED ARTIST AND ARCHITECT, Woolford undertook a pair of important paintings of Government House and many Atlantic Canadian landmarks during the tenure of Lord Dalhousie. Born in London, England in 1778, he was likely trained as an artist in the Drawing Room of the Board of Ordinance in the Tower of London. He served in the Royal Artillery and fought in the Napoleonic wars in continental Europe and Egypt. His painting skills were eventually recognized by Lord Dalhousie, a great patron of the arts, and he became the peer's artist in residence.

Woolford travelled to Canada when Dalhousie was appointed as lieutenant governor of Nova Scotia and would serve as "Draughtsman to His Excellency." He undertook many landscape paintings of Nova Scotia and New Brunswick and travelled throughout Atlantic Canada with Dalhousie. When Dalhousie was appointed as governor general of Canada, Woolford remained in Halifax to oversee the completion of Dalhousie College building.

By 1823 he relocated to Saint John, New Brunswick, where he would serve as architect to the British Army. Woolford's greatest achievement was his design of Government House Fredericton and King's College — what is today part of the University of New Brunswick.

BELOW: *View of Halifax from George's Island*

General, Solicitor General, Deputy Commissary General and Military Secretary.
The Reverend Robert Stanser, Rector of St. Paul's and the other clergymen, the Magistrates and principal Inhabitants of the Town &c.
Mr. Isaac Hildrith, Architect
Mr. John Henderson, Chief Mason.

ESTO PERPETUA

Immediately after laying the stone the Reverend Rector of St. Paul's concluded the ceremonies with the following prayer:--
Except the Lord build the house their labour is but lots that build it. Except the Lord keep the city, the watchmen walketh but in vain — 127th Psal., 1 & 2 verses.

LET US PRAY

O most merciful and gracious God, who preserveth and upholdeth all things by the word of Thy power, send down, we humbly beseech Thee, a blessing upon the present undertaking, and grant that this monument of the increasing prosperity of this infant colony may hand down to the latest prosperity the loyal and attachment of its inhabitants to the best of Sovereigns and their affection and regard for those who were at that period placed in authority under him, that by a steady adherence to the principles of our most excellent constitution, our children's children may enjoy the estimable privileges which Thy almighty protection had been secured to us till time itself shall be no more. Accept O Lord, our gratitude and thanks, and hear our petitions for Christ's sake. Amen.[49]

The participants and dignitaries, dressed in their finery, wigs and uniforms, returned to the old Government House for a cold lunch buffet — it would seem that despite Sir John's complaints about the structure, it was still serviceable. This would not be the last of the official entertainment to transpire at old Government House, which despite its condition, remained the official residence until late in 1805. While Sir John no longer permanently resided there, regular meetings of the Governor's Council and formal entertainments continued to be hosted within its wooden walls.

The challenges that befell the project and tribulations endured by Sir John Wentworth and the young province over the period of construction and finishing of the building are well worth considering, given they all came to influence the completion of Government House. While the legislature had authorized the expenditure of £10,500 for the land and construction of the building, the funding ran out by 1802 and Wentworth had to request additional funds to complete the project. Thenceforth, every year up to 1807, the lieutenant governor applied for additional funds to complete the new Government House. So outraged was the Legislature at the persistent cost overruns that they passed resolutions blaming Michael Wallace, the Chief Commissioner of the project, and the other Commissioners of Works for mismanaging the project and demanding their resignation. Alas for the poor members of the Legislature, this was the era of "irresponsible government" when the lieutenant governor was not required to act upon the protestations of the elected representatives. Wentworth blithely replied "The Commissioners appointed by me, for the building a Government-House, pursuant to the Law made for that purpose, being fully competent to that duty, and not having signified to me any intention to relinquish the trust reposed in them, and having hitherto conducted themselves in that service to my satisfaction, I see no necessity for the appointment of any others."[50] The Legislature again raised concerns in 1807; however, by this point the project was nearing completion, and by 1808, £22,000 had been expended on the structure, its interior finishes and some furnishings. By 1820 the total cost of the building, its upkeep (there seem to have been serious problems with the slate roof) and furnishings came to £31,659, 6 shillings and 8 pence. The expenditure would be something that clouded Wentworth's otherwise exceptional legacy.

The Wentworths would at last move into the building in the fall of 1805; however, work continued apace on the interior finishes and the grounds. Hildrith's tenure as architect and master builder came to a formal end of 31 December 1806, but work on the building would continue into 1807. Sir John's dream of a stately English country estate as the centre of official and social life in the young province of Nova Scotia having been realized — with a certain degree of personal cost, Wentworth's time as lieutenant governor concluded in 1808. In the words of Wentworth's biographer, Government House stands to this day as "a fitting monument to his taste and persistence."[51] Sir John would retire to his country estate on the Bedford Basin after a lifetime of service to King and country. His departure from vice-regal office did not mark his disappearance from civic life as he remained a fixture at many official events until his death in 1820 at the age of 83. Wentworth would be followed by Lieutenant General Sir George Prevost, a military man of Huguenot stock, who had been born in New Jersey and came to make Britain his home. Prevost's arrival came at a fortuitous juncture in the history of Nova Scotia and Canada — war with the United States was on the horizon. It would be Prevost who put the military affairs of Nova Scotia, and later all British North America, into proper order in preparation for the unhappy conflagration. Shortly after arriving at Government House Halifax, Prevost, who had lived the modest life of an untitled military officer, noted he had taken up "residence in an edifice out of all proportion to the situation." To Prevost, the building was far grander than was required for Britain's modest Nova Scotian province.

GOVERNOR'S FIELD & GOVERNOR'S FARM

Attached to Government House were a number of pieces of land that were used for farming. One of these, Governor's Field, occasionally referred to as Governor's Garden, was located adjacent to the Old Burying Ground, where Dalhousie University today has a number of buildings. Shortly after the building of Government House commenced, £500 was spent on acquiring a strip of land that allowed access to this property which would come to house stables for the governor's horses, a makeshift conservatory and a one-storey cottage for the gardener. It is known that a few cows and chickens were kept on this property for use by the governor and his household. In addition to this piece of land there was also 80 acres of land known as Governor's Farm, which was located along the shore of Halifax Harbour where Fort Needham was built and Mulgrave Park is today. This land had originally been used as a summer camp for the Mi'kmaq on account of the local spring.[52]

The province and the city of Halifax were anxious to gain control over these prime pieces of land. The province wanted Governor's Farm as it was located in a section of the city where the Inter-Colonial Railway would cut through, and it was ideal for development.

GENERAL SIR JOHN PREVOST, BT (1767–1816)

THE DEFENDER OF CANADA during the War of 1812, Prevost is one of four lieutenant governors of Nova Scotia who went on to become governor general of Canada. The son of a French-speaking Swiss Protestant who was a senior officer in the British Army, Prevost was born in New Jersey and would go on to serve in various posts throughout the West Indies and Britain. Prevost held the appointment as Governor of Dominica from 1802 to 1805 and would serve as Nova Scotia's lieutenant governor from 1808 to 1811, succeeding the first resident of Government House, Sir John Wentworth. Prevost attempted to see the military fortifications of the province improved and secured a new Militia Act, which helped to supplement the British Army in the region during a period of rising tensions with the United States.

During his service as Lieutenant Governor, Prevost was called upon to serve as second in command for an expedition to the island of Martinique, which resulted in the British capturing the island. His approach to legislative matters did much to improve relations between the governor and the elected representatives, even having success in imposing a liquor tax to cover the cost of the provincial militia. In the fall of 1811, Prevost was commissioned as Governor-in-Chief of British North America and he would play a central role in the War of 1812.

In March 1815, following the successful conclusion of the War, Prevost was replaced as governor general and died early in 1816 at the age of 48. An elegant set of sterling silver wine coolers and a coffee urn, presented to Prevost upon his retirement as lieutenant governor, are on permanent display in the Dining Room.

The interest in Governor's Field is less obvious; however, being the only large undeveloped plot of land in the downtown core that was not owned by the British government, it was no doubt alluring. An unusual deal was struck for these pieces of real estate; the land was surrendered to the provincial board of works "for the benefit of the province, to be used, leased, sold or conveyed, in whole or in part."[53] As compensation for the land, the provincial board of works agreed to pay for "lighting, water and warming of government house: provided that the sum so expended shall not, in any one year, exceed two hundred pounds."[54] This agreement to compensate the lieutenant governor, "In lieu of Farm" as it was listed in the Public Accounts, remained in place until 1901, when the annual payment of $778.66 (£200) came to an end. By this point Governor's Farm had been subdivided and sold; however, Governor's Field remained the property of the province — and it would seem successive lieutenant governors continued to use parts of it for agricultural purposes!

THE ADDRESS

WHEN CONSTRUCTION BEGAN on Government House the front entrance faced Hollis Street, while the service entrance was off Pleasant Street directly across from the Old Burying Ground. Interestingly, Pleasant Street was the very same name as the street upon which Sir John's family home in Portsmouth, New Hampshire, stood. By the time Sir John and Lady Wentworth took up residence in the stately home late in 1805, the address was simply "Government House, Halifax." As the town grew into a city, numbering was introduced, and the building was assigned the address "321 Pleasant Street."

With the construction of the new Ocean Terminals at the foot of South Street, beginning in 1913, there was a movement towards rationalizing a number of street names. The city decided to consolidate four street names into one: Barrington, Campbell, Lockman and Pleasant were merged into modern day Barrington Street. In the summer of 1917 new street signs were erected and the Government House address became "321 Barrington Street." This change also made sense as Pleasant Street no longer led to Point Pleasant Park, as it had since the establishment of the Park. Following the end of the Second World War, as the population of Canada expanded, the Post Office Department began encouraging larger metropolitan centres to introduce a rationalized, grid based numbering system, this to make the mail delivery system more efficient. In February 1965, the City of Halifax changed the address to its present designation "1451 Barrington Street."

The street where Government House sits was surveyed shortly after the British arrived in 1749. It was Charles Morris who undertook the initial survey, and it was likely he who made "the first clerical error in this government town,"[55] given that the name of the street was almost certainly to have been in honour of the Earl of Harrington, who was Lord Lieutenant of Ireland at the time. The letter "H" having been mistaken for a "B" in the cursive handwriting of the period is entirely plausible.

BELOW: *Map of Government House and adjacent property*

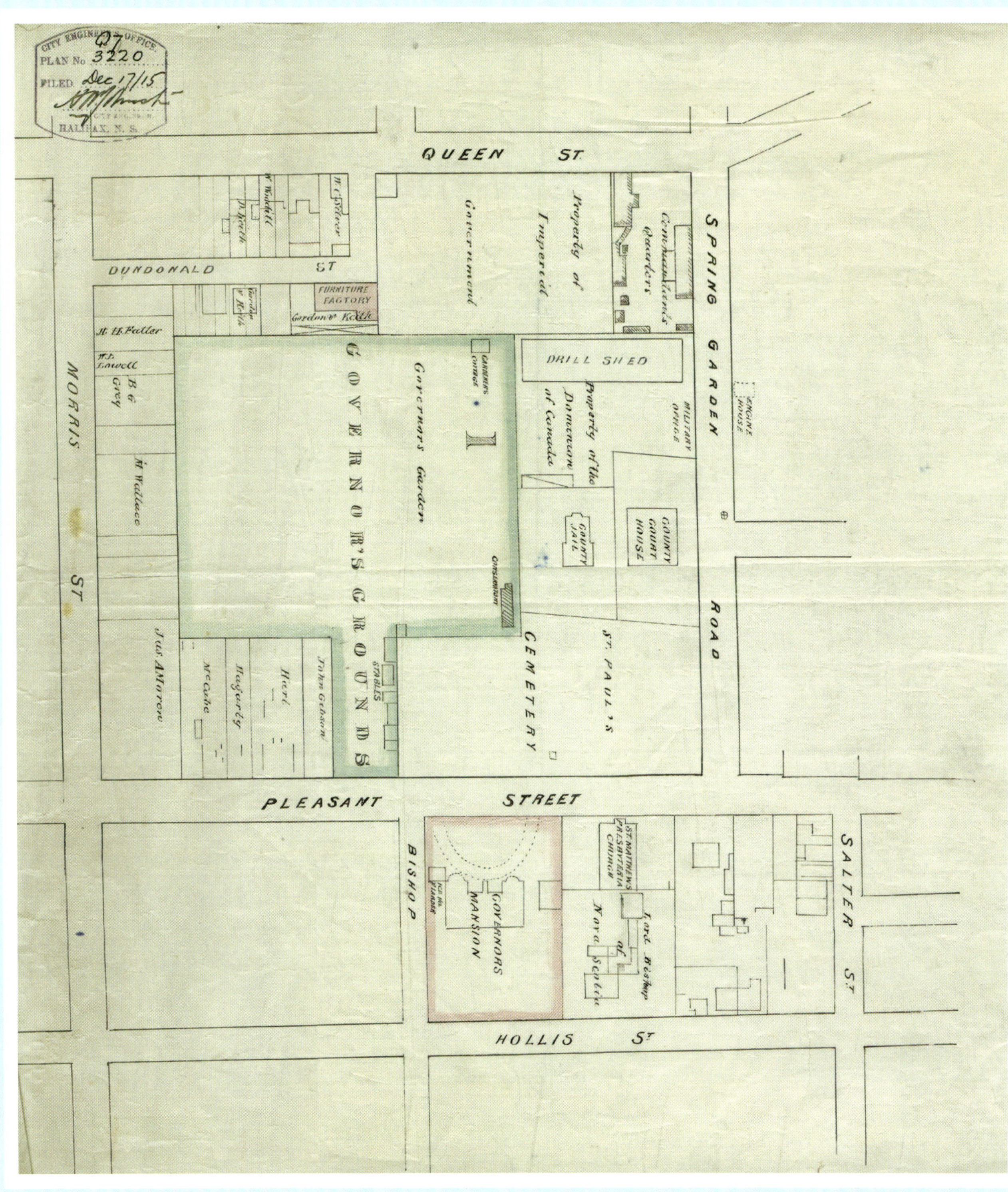

The Lieutenant Governor having received a Letter from Brigadier General Ogilvie Commander in Chief of His Majesty's Forces in this Province, stating that he finds it necessary for the good of His Majesty's service to purchase a Quantity of Spirits for the use of the Regiments now under Order to embark for the Island of Jamaica, not exceeding Two Thousand Gallons, and requesting that the same may be exempted from Provincial Duty, upon the ground of all Spirits and Wine purchased for the use of His Majesty's Troops being exempted from Duty in Great Britain: the Lieutenant Governor therefore recommends it to the House of Assembly to adopt such measure as shall be proper for granting the exemption requested.

J Wentworth.

Council Chamber
7th July 1792.

VERSO: *Order signed by Sir John Wentworth*

FOUR

A Place of Government and Home of the Lieutenant Governor

GOVERNMENT HOUSE IS the setting where the many different facets of the lieutenant governor's role and function converge. It is not just the ceremonial home, it is where the dignified and efficient work of government is transacted; it has a central place in both the formal ceremonial and constitutional aspects of how a constitutional monarchy functions, but it also, like the Crown itself, has a convening function, to bring diverse peoples together to be recognized, celebrated, and remembered.

In 1805, when Sir John Wentworth took up residence in Government House, the building was the hub of all government activity in the province. The legislature had no permanent seat and served largely as an advisory body for the governor, rather than its modern role as the forum where laws are proposed and debated by the democratically elected representatives of the people. The lieutenant governor carried out a varied array of responsibilities that are now discharged by different office holders. Along with serving as the King's representative and delegate of the British government, the lieutenant governor was commander-in-chief of the military forces, acted as the premier, head of the civil service and mayor of Halifax. Over the fifty years following the completion of Government House, these roles would be recast and assigned to different officials. With this, our modern system of democratic government was developed and refined.

Today, as The Queen's home in the province and the residence of the lieutenant governor, Government House continues to be the place where various aspects of the Crown's role in our system of government frequently take place. As a constitutional monarchy and federal parliamentary democracy, the head of state is The Queen of Canada, who is represented at the federal level by the governor general, and in each of the ten provinces by a lieutenant governor. Each lieutenant governor is appointed by the governor general and by a commission issued in the name of The Queen, all on the advice of the prime minister. Lieutenant governors serve in office for not less than five years, although some have served for upwards of a decade, while a few

ABOVE: *Her Majesty Queen Elizabeth II, Queen of Canada*

BELOW: *Sir John Harvey*

in the world, the United Kingdom and United States being the two oldest.

There are also certain circumstances in which the lieutenant governor can act without receiving formal advice from the premier, notably following a general election where no political party holds a majority of the seats. The lieutenant governor must always ensure that the province has a premier; if the position becomes vacant for any reason, the lieutenant governor will select a member of the legislature to become premier, normally the person commanding the most number of seats in the legislature.

Like The Queen, the lieutenant governor does not get involved in politics or the policy decisions of the government of the day; the lieutenant governor is always supposed to act above the political fray. In his or her interactions with the premier, the lieutenant governor has the right to be consulted, to encourage and to warn. In this capacity the lieutenant governor meets at Government House privately, on a regular basis, with the premier.

Until 1876, the lieutenant governor also chaired meetings of the Executive Council (Cabinet); however, vice-regal participation in Cabinet deliberations ceased long ago, as it is not appropriate for the Crown's representative to be involved in the policy decisions of the government of the day. There was also a time when the lieutenant governor served as the representative of the federal government in the province; however, this aspect of the vice-regal role also came to end a long time ago.[56] In extraordinary circumstances, the lieutenant governor may also refuse to grant Royal Assent to a bill, or to reserve or disallow a bill. These prerogatives continue to exist, although they have not been exercised for more than half a century in Canada. Reserve power allows the lieutenant governor to withhold Royal Assent to a bill and await the approval of the governor general, which would be exercised by the Federal government.

The lieutenant governor can also refuse Royal Assent. The last time either of these powers were used was 1883, by the long-serving lieutenant governor of the day Sir Adams George Archibald, himself a former attorney general.[57]

Nova Scotia was at the forefront of the development of democracy in Canada. With the attainment of Representative Government in 1758, and then in 1848 the achievement of Responsible Government, the Crown and its representative, the lieutenant governor, have played a central part in the development of our system of government. Not surprisingly, many of these key moments have taken place at Government House.

One of the most memorable occurred in the early months of 1848. Lieutenant Governor Sir John Harvey accepted the resignation of the provincial cabinet on 28 January of that year, these being the last ministers of the Crown personally appointed by him. On the morning of 2 February, Sir John welcomed nine members of the House of Assembly into the Drawing Room: James B. Uniacke, Michael Tobin, Hugh Bell, Joseph Howe, James McNab, Herbert Huntington, William F. DesBarres, Lawrence O'Connor Doyle and George R. Young. Here he swore them in as members of the provincial cabinet, administering the oath of allegiance and of office to each of them. With this the

THE HONOURABLE SIR ADAMS GEORGE ARCHIBALD, PC, KCMG, QC (1814–1892)

BORN IN TRURO, Archibald would go on to a distinguished career as a lawyer, politician and as lieutenant governor of two provinces. Although he initially trained as a medical doctor, he found the profession uninteresting and studied law. A lawyer of some note, he was appointed a judge in 1848 and also helped to oversee the construction of an electric telegraph system from Halifax to New Brunswick. Later, as a Member of the Legislative Assembly, Archibald served as Solicitor General and would represent Nova Scotia at the Quebec and then the London Conferences, making him a Father of Confederation. He would serve as an MP in the first Dominion Parliament and be appointed Secretary of State for the Provinces (Intergovernmental Affairs Minister) until 1870.

Archibald served as the first lieutenant governor of Manitoba for the initial two years after that province entered Confederation, and he did much to try to quell the tension between the Métis and anglophone settlers in the province. He served briefly as a Justice of the Supreme Court of Nova Scotia, then, following the untimely death of Joseph Howe, he succeeded his anti-Confederation foe as lieutenant governor for an entire decade, from 1873 to 1883. He was the last lieutenant governor to chair meetings of the Executive Council (Cabinet), and having been deeply experienced with the development of Responsible Government, he undertook similar measures to distance the Queen's representative from being directly involved in the politics and policy of the government of the day.

He helped found the Dalhousie law school and to expand the university and was also a founding member of the Nova Scotia Historical Society. After leaving Government House, Archibald returned briefly to federal politics as a Member of Parliament, sitting from 1888 to 1891, and he died the following year.

first cabinet responsible to the legislature and the voters of Nova Scotia took office.

Still to the present day the lieutenant governor presides over the swearing-in of members of the Executive Council (Cabinet), often at Government House. There are also the regular meetings that take place between the lieutenant governor and the premier, which are modelled on the weekly meetings that take place between The Queen and the prime minister of the United Kingdom. Each year the lieutenant governor, as the Crown's representative in the province, hosts a meeting of the provincial cabinet, thereby bringing the main actors in our system of Responsible Government home to where our system of democracy was first practised. Other significant functions which the lieutenant governor undertakes at Government House includes the signing of pardons, such as that granted to the late Grand Chief Gabriel Sylliboy in 2017, and the more routine business of reviewing and signing orders-in-council, appointments, land grants and vice-regal warrants for the expenditure of funds from the provincial treasury. Several times a week the Clerk of the Executive Council, who is head of the provincial public service and deputy minister to the premier, has an audience with the lieutenant governor to review the necessary state papers, which are an integral part of the operation of our democracy.

There is a symmetry to many of the events that take place within Government House. One of the more solemn ceremonies took place on 22 January 1936, two days following the death of King George v. The King, who had spent time at Government House both as a young sailor in the Royal Navy and later in 1901 during the famed Empire-wide Royal Tour of the Duke and

GENERAL THE HONOURABLE SIR WILLIAM FENWICK WILLIAMS, BT, GCB (1800–1883)

BORN AT ANNAPOLIS ROYAL, Williams would rise to the pinnacle of military and civil accomplishment in the British Empire. Being from a military family, Williams attended the Royal Military Academy at Woolwich in England and would serve in the Royal Artillery in Ceylon (Sri Lanka), Turkey, Iran and most notably in the Crimean War. When the war broke out in 1854, Williams was assigned a leading role in reorganizing the Turkish Army, and he would gain fame as the hero of the Battle of Kars, despite losing the battle to the Russians. The defence he led at Kars made him a hero of the Crimean War; he was knighted, awarded an annual pension of £1,000 and was even elected to the British Parliament, sitting as an MP from 1856 to 1859. He would then be commissioned as Commander-in-Chief of British forces in North America on the eve the American Civil War. Appointed as lieutenant governor of his native Nova Scotia in 1865, he would serve as the Queen's representative until October 1867.

Williams was perhaps the first truly internationally famous Nova Scotian. In 1870 he was appointed Governor and Commander-in-Chief of Gibraltar, where he served until 1876. He died in London in 1881. Widely rumoured to be an illegitimate son of Prince Edward, Duke of Kent, Williams revelled in the suggestion that he was Queen Victoria's half-brother, although in recent times it has been proven that he was not a relative of the Duke of Kent.

ABOVE: *The Queen and her Provincial Executive Council (Cabinet), 2010*

BELOW LEFT: *Lieutenant Governor J.J. Grant addressing a meeting of the Executive Council c. 2013*

BELOW RIGHT: *Dropping of the Writ, Lieutenant Governor J.J. Grant signing the Order and Proclamation dissolving the Provincial Legislature and calling a general election, 2017*

ABOVE: *Premier Angus L. Macdonald signing the accession proclamation in the Drawing Room, 1936*

BELOW LEFT: *Lieutenant Governor J.J. Grant delivering the Speech from the Throne, 2014*

BELOW RIGHT: *Lieutenant Governor James Cranswick Tory, at work in the Study, 1928*

BELOW: *Lieutenant Governor J.J. Grant laying a wreath at the War Memorial, Grand Parade Halifax, 2016*

Duchess of Cornwall and York, was a much beloved figure. Following the "demise of the Crown," it has been tradition for the new Sovereign to be proclaimed and for all those holding Crown offices to swear an oath of allegiance to the new Sovereign. Following George V's death, the lieutenant governor, chief justice, premier, clerk of the Executive Council and private secretary to the lieutenant governor gathered in the Drawing Room to witness the proclamation of the new King, which was read by the clerk of the Executive Council after it was received from Ottawa, and then to swear allegiance to King Edward VIII.[58]

THE DIGNIFIED ROLE: CEREMONIAL & SOCIAL PROCEEDINGS

The ceremonial and social role, which makes up the convening power of the Crown, is equally broad. In essence, the lieutenant governor serves as the non-partisan "promoter-in-chief" of the province and its people, presenting honours and awards; recognizing volunteers; representing all Nova Scotians at state events such as Victoria Day, Canada Day, the Fête Nationale de l'Acadie, Treaty Day celebrations, the installation of the governor general; welcoming members of the Royal Family; and greeting visiting Commonwealth and foreign diplomats and visiting senior military officers.

ABOVE: *Mi'kmaq drummers with the original Treaty of Peace and Friendship, following a ceremony in 2016*

BELOW: *Pardon granted to the late Grand Chief Gabriel Sylliboy*

For other events, such as funerals, memorials and Remembrance Day, the lieutenant governor serves as the "mourner-in-chief" and represents all Nova Scotians by participating in these occasions when citizens come together to mark important passings.

Two other aspects of the lieutenant governor's role can be found in the relationship the Crown has with Indigenous peoples and with the Canadian Armed Forces. The Crown's connection with the Indigenous people of Canada is deeply woven into our history and is also a legal reality. The various treaties between the Crown-in-Right of Canada and the Mi'kmaq people, who have lived in Nova Scotia since ancient times, remain an important aspect of Canada's constitution and have gained greater importance in the era of reconciliation. Chief amongst these are the various

Treaties of Peace and Friendship of 1725, 1752, and 1761 and the Royal Proclamation of 1763. The lieutenant governor attends pow wows throughout the province every year, and welcomes Mi'kmaq leaders to Government House to celebrate Treaty Day and other significant events. Many ceremonies held at Government House are opened by a ceremonial smudging and performances by Mi'kmaq drummers and dancers.

The military has always had a special relationship with the Crown, dating back to the establishment of Acadia and New France. To this day, members of the military swear an oath of allegiance to the Sovereign, and The Queen serves as titular head of all the military forces in Canada. Up until the time of Confederation in 1867, many lieutenant governors exercised a military function as well as their role in the government of the province. Indeed, Nova Scotia's first post-Confederation lieutenant governor, Sir William Fenwick Williams, served as commander-in-chief in and over Canada during his time as lieutenant governor. Since 1905, the commander-in-chief role has been vested in the governor general. Although there is no longer a constitutional military function, as the Crown's representative in the province, the lieutenant governor presides over various change of command ceremonies and graduation parades and welcomes numerous Commonwealth and foreign military officers to the province each year. As home to the largest military base in the country, and to more military personnel than in any other province, this longstanding relationship constitutes an important part of the lieutenant governor's annual activities.

The first recorded great event to take place on the site where Government House today stands was the laying of the cornerstone of the building on 11 September 1800. The Old Burying Ground, what was at the time the cemetery of St. Paul's Church, directly across the street from Government House, was witness to many a noted burial in the period prior to the construction of the building, and it is likely that, long before Europeans arrived in Nova Scotia, the Mi'kmaq may have conducted ceremonies in the general vicinity where Government House now stands.

LIEUTENANT COLONEL WILLIAM BRUCE ALMON, RCA (1875–1961)

DESCENDENT OF THE FIRST LOYALISTS to arrive in Nova Scotia, W.B. Almon was a professional soldier who would serve as an officer in the Royal Canadian Artillery. Almon spent much of the First World War in Halifax and played a role in the post-Halifax Explosion recovery efforts as one of the senior most officers in the city at the time of the disaster. Following the end of the war in Europe, Almon saw service as a member of the Canadian Siberian Expeditionary Force. From 1924 to early 1943 Almon was private secretary to the lieutenant governor and was the second longest-serving holder of the post, just behind Lieutenant-Colonel Holt W. Clerke (1877–1900). A man of many facets, beyond his military and vice-regal service, Almon was involved with early theatre in Nova Scotia and was a well-known figure in Halifax society of the period.

VERSO: *The Duke of Kent, father of Queen Victoria*

FIVE

Royal Residents and Vice-Regal Visitors

PRIOR TO THE PRESENT Government House being erected, Nova Scotia had a history of welcoming various members of the Royal family to the province. Queen Victoria's father, Prince Edward Augustus, Duke of Kent, lived in the province from 1794 until 1800, and during the last part of his residency he served as Commander-in-Chief of British forces in North America. His brother Prince William Henry, Duke of Gloucester, spent time at Government House in the fall of 1784 and developed much more than just a very close friendship with Lady Wentworth.

Since the Wentworths moved into Government House in 1805, the building has welcomed more members of the Royal Family than any residence in the Western Hemisphere, other than perhaps Rideau Hall in Ottawa. The building has been the home-away-from-home for numerous Royals and has welcomed many governors general, governors, lieutenant governors and Commonwealth and foreign dignitaries. Halifax being a military centre, there has been a constant flow of senior military officers visiting Government House; this was especially true during the two world wars of the last century. Appendix One chronicles the various Royal visitors to Nova Scotia.

The pinnacle event held at Government House has always been to host a visit undertaken by a member or members of the Royal Family. One of the most memorable took place in 1860, when Queen Victoria's eldest son, His Royal Highness Albert Edward, Prince of Wales (the future King Edward VII), undertook a tour of British North America and the United States, during which he spent two days in residence at Government House. The Prince's visit to Nova Scotia was certainly the grandest state event to take place in the province until the post-Confederation period. A massive welcome procession greeted the Prince, made up of government officials, various loyal societies, Mi'kmaq leaders, representatives of the African Abolition Society and the general public.

The provincial government voted £2,000 to upgrade the furnishings and decoration of the official residence, and this included the addition of rococo gilt window valances displaying the Prince of Wales's feathers and

ABOVE: *The Royal Tour 1860, Albert Prince of Wales holding a levée in the Drawing Room*

BELOW: *Gilt valance displaying the Prince of Wales's feathers*

four massive rococo gilt French mirrors for the Drawing Room, decorations that remain in place to this day. To defray at least part of the expense of the tour the province would spend on the visit, tickets were sold for the ball held in honour of the Prince of Wales, generating £1,000. Neighbouring New Brunswick, with a population almost half that of Nova Scotia, would spend a whopping £9,000[59] on hosting His Royal Highness, and cleverly sold off much of the furniture and china used by the Prince to cover the costs associated with the visit.

The most significant event to take place during the 1860 Royal Tour was a levée held in the Drawing Room beginning at 11 am on 1 August, at which more than two thousand people were introduced to His Royal Highness, and even the *New York Times* noted "it cannot be said there was any uneasy stiffness about the affair."[60] The Prince was notably presented with a cigar case of Mi'kmaq quillwork "beautifully worked in slips of different coloured bead ornaments"[61] by Mi'kmaq leaders wearing the Indian Chief Medals that had been presented to their ancestors during the reign of King George III. The evening was taken up by a state dinner in honour of the Prince of Wales followed by a fireworks display. The visit remained in the minds of Nova Scotians for many years after, with His Royal Highness donating the Prince of Wales Cup, establishing the Prince of Wales Regatta and becoming a patron of the Royal Nova Scotia Yacht Squadron.

As transatlantic travel became increasingly easy, members of the Royal Family made their way to Canada with regularity. The end of the Victorian era brought the Duke and Duchess of Cornwall and York (the future King George V and Queen Mary), who travelled throughout the far-flung British Empire in 1901, aboard the HMS *Ophir*. The visit of the future King

LADY WENTWORTH (1745–1813)

AN ENIGMATIC and much talked-about figure, Frances Deering Wentworth was born into a wealthy and influential family. Known throughout her life as a grand hostess and lavish entertainer, she and Sir John became the centre of social life in Nova Scotia for nearly a quarter century. She was notably described as "a person of great beauty and accomplishment."[62]

First married at the age of 16, in 1762, to Theodore Atkinson, she was widowed in 1769. Two weeks later she would marry her first cousin John Wentworth on 11 November in Portsmouth, New Hampshire. So outraged were members of the Wentworth family at this union that Sir John would ultimately be disinherited by his uncle and parents. The Wentworths, with their deep Loyalist sensibilities, would serve on the British side during the American Revolution and would ultimately flee Portsmouth on 13 June 1775 when rebels aimed a cannon at the front door of their home on Pleasant Street.

As consort to the lieutenant governor of Nova Scotia, Frances was the consummate hostess. In one year alone "more than 2,500 people dined at Government House."[63] This included Prince Edward, Duke of Kent (father of Queen Victoria) during his time as Commander-in-Chief of British North America, and she and the Duke would become more than close friends. During an extended visit by Prince William Henry, Duke of Gloucester, one of Prince Edward's older brothers, she entered into a relationship with him. Indeed, both she and husband became known for their flexible sexual mores, and "the wild life at Government House."

Lady Wentworth was presented at Court to King George III and Queen Charlotte in 1798 and would subsequently be appointed Lady-in-Waiting to Her Majesty The Queen "with permission to reside abroad." She would die at the age of 68 at Sunninghill, Berkshire, England in 1813, leaving behind Sir John and their one son, Sir Charles Mary Wentworth Bt (1775–1844).

LEFT: *The Duke and Duchess of Cornwall and York as displayed on a commemorative plate*

RIGHT: *Parade in honour of the 1901 Royal Tour of the Duke and Duchess of Cornwall and York*

and Queen brought about some significant changes to the second floor of Government House, including the creation of a Royal Bedroom out of the Saloon, and the modernization of the bathroom facilities. The Duke had visited Government House in 1883 as a nineteen-year-old officer in the Royal Navy. One of the more poignant moments in the 1901 Royal Tour came when the Duke noticed an older gentleman amongst a parade of veterans wearing the Victoria Cross along with a number of other campaign medals. Anxious to find out more, His Royal Highness engaged in a lengthy conversation with William Hall, the first Nova Scotian and the first person of African descent to earn Britain's highest gallantry decoration. Hall, who had never made a fuss about his service, was almost entirely unrecognized by his fellow Canadians until His Royal Highness drew attention to Hall's outstanding service. In a period when racism against African-Nova Scotians was endemic, having the future King take an interest in a forgotten hero no doubt caused some consternation amongst some of Halifax's elite, but it made an important point about the ability of any person, regardless of background, to commit an

BELOW: *William Hall, VC*

ABOVE: *Painting of William Hall's Victoria Cross action*

BELOW: *Prince Albert (future King George VI)*

act of bravery. Upon their departure from Nova Scotia, the Duke of Cornwall and York noted in his diary on 19 October, "at 7:45 we dined with the Lt Governor & Mrs. Jones, 65 people. At 1000 we held a reception in the Provincial Building and shook hands with 622 people. We got on board [HMS *Ophir*] at 11:30, still blowing and raining."[64]

In honour of King George V's coronation in 1911, Lieutenant Governor James Drummond McGregor and his wife Elizabeth held a lavish Coronation reception and dance which involved more than 400 guests. Members of the cabinet, chief justice, senior army and naval officers and a bevy of diplomatic representatives including the German, French, Norwegian and Portuguese Consuls along with the American Consul General were in attendance.[65] Officers from the British cruiser HMS *Cornwall* and the German Imperial Navy's cruiser SMS *Bremen* were also in attendance. Mrs. McGregor oversaw the preparations, and each room on the main floor of Government House was festooned with floral decorations and palm leaves. Hospitality was provided throughout the main floor of the house, while the west

ABOVE: *King George VI and Queen Elizabeth flanked by members of the RCMP during the 1939 Royal Tour, rear entrance of Government House*

MIDDLE: *Queen Elizabeth The Queen Mother leaving Government House to present a new Queen's Colour to Maritime Command (Royal Canadian Navy), 1979*

BELOW: *1976 Royal Tour Luncheon menu cover*

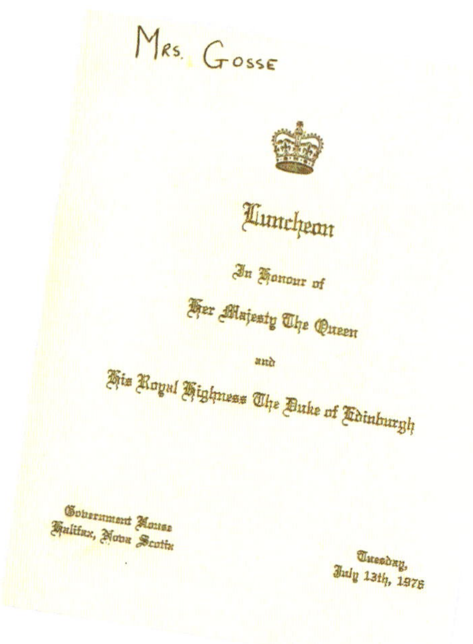
Mrs. Gosse

Luncheon

In Honour of

Her Majesty The Queen

and

His Royal Highness The Duke of Edinburgh

Government House
Halifax, Nova Scotia

Tuesday,
July 13th, 1976

end of the Ballroom was set up with an orchestra, the windows being flung open to carry the music into the garden where guests enjoyed dancing and refreshments in one of two large marquees that had been set up on the lawn. It was an unconventional event when one considers the number of guests, opening of the entire main floor of the house and indoor-outdoor nature of the celebrations.

As a seventeen-year-old naval cadet, Prince Albert, the future King George VI, was welcomed to Government House with a tea and dance in his honour with two hundred guests. "One look at the Prince won everyone's heart, for the ingenuousness of the boy made all feel that he rebelled against the ostentatious display that the occasion demanded … at the Government House reception … he ingratiated himself in the hearts of all by his unceasing efforts to make pleasure for others."[66] In 1939 the young prince would return, this time as King George VI and would be accompanied by his consort Queen Elizabeth, as part of the famous 1939 Royal Tour, the first visit of a reigning Sovereign to Canada. Their Majesties were in residence at Government House during the Halifax portion of their tour in June of that year. Queen Elizabeth, as Queen Mother, would return on a number of occasions, most notably in 1979 to present a new Queen's Colour to Maritime Command (subsequently re-designated as the Royal Canadian Navy) and to open the International Gathering of the Clans. She also inaugurated what would become the Royal Nova Scotia International Tattoo.

Three months before the death of her father, King George VI, Princess Elizabeth and Prince Philip made a five-week, cross-Canada tour which included an overnight stay at Government House in Halifax. The table which Their Royal Highnesses used to sign the official guest book was donated to Government House in 2011. With official visits to Province House, Dalhousie University and Royal Canadian Navy installations, the Royal Couple then made their way to Cape Breton for a

INSET: *Larry Freeman, QC, first male vice-regal consort*

THE CONSORTS

THE ROLE OF THE VICE-REGAL CONSORT, sometimes referred to as the "chatelaine," has not been well recorded by historians, yet it is unquestionably a significant position within our understanding of the lieutenant governor's role. To this day, the vice-regal consort continues to play an important part in supporting the lieutenant governor in their myriad of ceremonial and social duties, not unlike the support given to the Sovereign by their consort.

In the period prior to the 1950s, when the lieutenant governor covered the cost of most of the household staff and entertainment, the consort had a very direct role in the running of the household. She oversaw the management of the servants, the planning and execution of social events and also had a preeminent position within Nova Scotian society, especially amongst the Halifax elite. The highly gendered roles of the two sexes that emerged during the Victorian era further entrenched this approach, with women largely responsible for the home and events that took place within it and men involved in the outside world. Government House, however, provided a unique environment where the public and private worlds naturally came together, and thus it was advantageous for the consorts to be adept at not only running an efficient and elegant official residence along with hosting a myriad of high-profile social events, but also serving as the principal support and promoter of their husbands. In a period when women were not able to vote or hold office, they nevertheless found other avenues for involvement well beyond simply holding fancy parties. Status and station were reflective and it is certain that many lieutenant governors owed a great deal of their own success to their wives. With the professionalization of the household staff, the management responsibilities for the overall operation of Government House have been assumed by the private secretary.

There is little question that the first vice-regal consort to live in Government House, Lady Wentworth, was a social force and very much an equal partner to her husband in all of the entertainment and events held at the residence. Some governors, notably those from a military background, did not have, or bring with them, a spouse and were left to undertake the various social duties solo, accompanied only by an aide-de-camp and or their private secretary. Until the appointment of Myra Freeman in 2000, every vice-regal consort in Nova Scotia had been a female — Lawrence Freeman becoming the first male consort. Mayann Francis was the first lieutenant governor since Sir Charles Hastings Doyle to take up office without a consort. While there was a time when being single would have precluded appointment to the province's highest office, this is no longer the case.

It was only in 1985 that the lieutenant governor's consort was accorded the courtesy style "Her Honour," Rose Abraham becoming the first resident of Government House to be so styled. This change helped to recognize the important role played by vice-regal consorts and their contribution to supporting and enabling the Crown's representative to discharge the many public duties in a multifaceted manner. The consort or spouse plays a significant support role, and often serves as patron of a number of organizations, although they are not accorded any constitutional functions.

ABOVE: *The Queen and the Royal Tour staff at Government House, 1959*

BELOW LEFT: *1959 Royal Tour Dinner invitation*

BELOW RIGHT: *Brooch presented by The Queen to Mrs. Mary Plow during 1959 Royal Tour*

Their Royal Highnesses The Princess Elizabeth Duchess of Edinburgh and the Duke of Edinburgh
having graciously signified their intention to be present

The Lieutenant Governor and Mrs. McCurdy
request the pleasure of
Rear Admiral and Mrs. Mainguy's
company at dinner
on Wednesday the seventh of November
at a quarter to eight o'clock for eight o'clock

An answer is requested
to the Private Secretary
repeating the date and time

Black Tie miniatures

ABOVE: *The Queen rededicating Government House, 28 June 2010; Premier Darrel Dexter, Lieutenant Governor Mayann Francis and The Duke of Edinburgh look on*

MIDDLE: *The Queen's Plaque rededicating Government House, 2010*

BELOW: *The Queen and The Duke of Edinburgh walk up the Government House driveway past the Lieutenant Governor's Aides-de-Camp before departing Halifax, 30 June 2010*

visit to the steel mill and to the town of Sydney, aboard the destroyer HMCS *Crusader*.

Her Majesty Queen Elizabeth II would be in residence on multiple occasions, in 1959, 1976, 1994 and 2010. The Royal Tour of 1959 was most notable, given the fact that it was in the Dining Room at Government House where The Queen presided over a meeting of Her Canadian Privy Council (federal cabinet) when she approved the appointment of Major-General Georges Vanier as the first French Canadian governor general. During the 1994 Royal Tour The Queen helped commemorate the 175th anniversary of Province House and the Provincial Legislature, and during her 2010 Royal Tour The Queen and Duke of Edinburgh were in residence for two-and-a-half days. During their programme of extensive activities in Halifax, which ran from 28 to 30 June, the Royal Couple presided over the centennial of the Royal Canadian Navy with an international fleet review and rededicated Government House following the completion of the restoration, The Queen being presented with the Royal Key to Government House by Lieutenant Governor Mayann Francis. Then, the couple undertook a visit to a temporary Mi'kmaq village set up in honour of the 400th anniversary of the christening of Grand Chief Henri Membertou. His Royal Highness, as Colonel-in-Chief of the Royal Canadian Regiment, hosted a reception in honour of the Regiment in the Ballroom, and the Royal Couple also attended a number of cultural performances. The Queen's 2010 Royal Tour concluded with her departure from Government House with the playing of the Scottish tune *Will Ye No Come Back Again*, a particular favourite of The Queen Mother, which was also played during her last visit to Canada in 1989.

In 2014 the Prince of Wales returned to Government House, having last visited in 1983, although during that earlier visit His Royal Highness resided aboard the Royal Yacht *Britannia*. Accompanied by his consort, HRH The

VERSO: *The Queen departing Government House, 2010*

ABOVE AND MIDDLE: *The Prince of Wales being sworn in to the Queen's Privy Council for Canada*

BELOW: *Plaque commemorating the swearing-in ceremony*

Duchess of Cornwall, a diverse programme of events was carried out, including a private reception where Their Royal Highnesses met with the families of Canadian Armed Forces personnel who were killed in Afghanistan. Also, during this visit, His Royal Highness was sworn into The Queen's Privy Council for Canada by Governor General David Johnston. This dignified ceremony took place in the Drawing Room, the same room where Responsible Government was first exercised in 1848.

Over the last fifty years, other members of the Royal Family have also spent time at Government House. Princess Margaret, The Queen's sister, visited in 1958, and then in 1988 when she presented new Queen's and Regimental Colours to the Princess Louise Fusiliers. The Princess Royal visited in 1991 and was to make a second visit in 2014, but this was cancelled due to issues with trans-Atlantic flying caused by an erupting Icelandic volcano. The Duke of York opened the Royal Nova Scotia International Tattoo in 1985 and would return in 2009; however, on this last visit the restoration of Government House was not yet completed, so His Royal Highness stayed at an alternate location. The Earl of Wessex has visited frequently, first in 1987 to open the Royal Nova Scotia International Tattoo, then in 2000 to present Duke of Edinburgh Gold Awards and most recently in 2015. Prince Michael of Kent, youngest son of HRH Prince George Duke of Kent (who spent time in Nova Scotia at RCAF stations during the early part of the Second World War) visited Government House in 1984 when he came to mark the 75th anniversary of the flight of the Silver Dart, and then in 2002 when he returned for a private visit. Prince Michael's sister, Princess Alexandra, the Honourable Lady Ogilvy, visited Government House first in 1954 along with her mother Princess Marina, Duchess of Kent, and then in 1973 when she marked the 200th anniversary of the arrival of Scottish settlers in Pictou county and held a Garden Party at Government House.

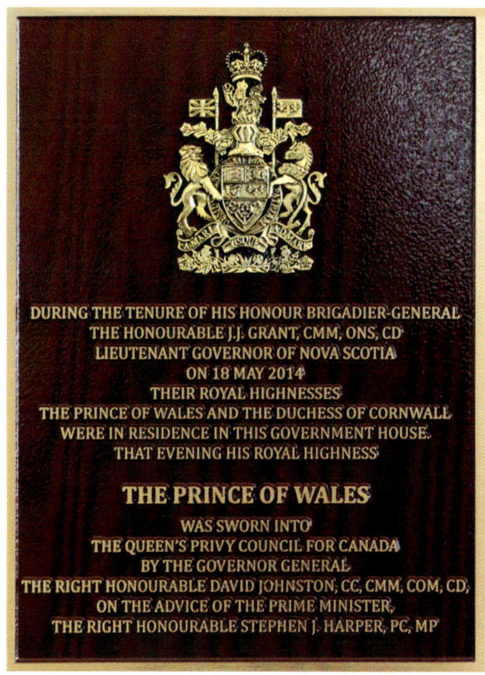

VICE-REGAL VISITORS

Since the time of Sir George Prevost, who served as lieutenant governor from 1808 to 1811, every governor general of Canada has visited and spent time at Government House over the course of their tenure. Halifax, as the most important port in Canada, was for many Governors General-designate their landing point upon arrival in Canada, and four of them would be sworn into office at Province House, with various other installation festivities taking place at Government House under the auspices of the lieutenant governor.[67] Four of Nova Scotia's lieutenant governors, and residents of Government House, went on to serve as governor general: Sir George Prevost (1812–15), Sir John Coape Sherbrooke (1816–18), Lord Dalhousie (1820–28) and Sir James Kempt (1828–30).

Of the various vice-regal visitors, one of the more important was Lord Sydenham, who was appointed as governor general of British North America shortly after the 1837 Rebellions in Upper and Lower Canada and was keen to quell the unrest that had spread throughout the Canadas. During a visit to Halifax in 1840, he stayed at Government House and here he met with Joseph Howe, a leading member of the reform movement. It was at this meeting that Howe passionately made Nova Scotia's case for Responsible Government. In 1873 upon their arrival in Canada, Lord and Lady Dufferin attended several events at Government House,

GENERAL THE RIGHT HONOURABLE LORD DALHOUSIE, GCB (1770–1838)

THE GREAT PATRON OF THE ARTS and military man — most remembered in Canada for his establishment of Dalhousie University — George Ramsay, 9th Earl of Dalhousie, was a Scottish peer, soldier and administrator who saw service around the globe.

The fifth official resident of Government House, Dalhousie's tenure as lieutenant governor, which lasted from 1816 to 1820, would be followed by his appointment as governor general of Canada from 1820 to 1828, and finally as Commander-in-Chief of British India from 1830 to 1832. Dalhousie distinguished himself in various military campaigns, with service in Gibraltar, the West Indies, Ireland and Europe, also having served under the Duke of Wellington. Shortly after arriving in Nova Scotia, he immediately set out to travel throughout the province, and on these excursions he brought his artist-in-residence, John Elliott Woolford, along to sketch and paint the topography and geography of the province over which he had responsibility.

Relations with the legislature were not always friendly, especially on matters related to the militia; however; he did much to accelerate the building of roads to improve commerce and defence. While he worked to alleviate the plight of black refugees from the War of 1812, his views on African-Nova Scotians and the Mi'kmaq were intolerant at best. He had a particular dislike for local merchants, whom he viewed as lacking sufficient competition and as gougers of the citizenry. Having grown up in an aristocratic family and served in the military, Dalhousie was keen on hierarchy and rank, and naturally it was the elite of Nova Scotian society who dominated the social scene during his and Lady Dalhousie's time at Government House.

ABOVE: *Countess of Aberdeen*

BELOW: *HRH the Duke of Edinburgh, Colonel-in-Chief of the Royal Canadian Regiment in a Regimental Photo with 2nd Battalion, RCR, June 2010.*

although they resided aboard their schooner yacht *Foam*, for the duration of their visit. The swearing in of the Marquess of Lorne as governor general, accompanied by his wife, HRH Princess Louise, daughter of Queen Victoria, was a particularly noteworthy occasion. The couple, accompanied by Prince Alfred, one of Queen's Victoria's sons who had previously visited Halifax in 1861 as a young naval Midshipman, was greeted by Sir John A. Macdonald and Lieutenant Governor Sir Adams James Archibald. The evening before the swearing-in ceremony at Province House, a state dinner was held at Government House in honour of the occasion, with the swearing-in taking place on 25 November 1878.

A visit by the Earl and Countess of Aberdeen was particularly memorable on account of the activist work undertaken by the Countess. Although not devoid of the usual ceremony and flummery associated with vice-regal visitors, it was under the Countess' direction that a meeting of the Local Council of Women was held in 1894, in connection with women's suffrage. Beginning with the election of the first Legislative Assembly in 1758, women in Nova Scotia who met a property qualification were able to vote in provincial elections; however, this right was removed from them in 1851. Through the 1890s the Local Council of Women worked to lobby politicians to restore their vote. The Countess was a force in the world of women's rights, serving variously as President of the International Women's Council and founder of the National Council for Women of Canada and the Victorian Order of Nurses. "The dining room of Government House was tastefully decorated with flowers for the occasions. A lovely vase placed on the table designed for Her Excellency the Countess of Aberdeen. The heads and delegates of the Halifax Society and some of the province were present."[68] As part of the social aspect of the vice-regal visit, the Aberdeens were guests of honour

BELOW: *Photo portrait of Princess Louise, Duchess of Connaught*

ABOVE: HRH *Prince Arthur, Duke of Connaught*

at a Government House garden party, the Countess noting "everything was as well done as they could be in London."[69]

Another of Queen Victoria's sons, Prince Arthur, Duke of Connaught, visited Halifax and Government House on multiple occasions, first in August 1869 and then in April 1906, as a senior military officer. In 1910 the Duke would be appointed governor general of Canada, and in 1912 he returned to Halifax, this time to unveil Sir Sanford Fleming Park and the Dingle Tower, travelling onward to visit Digby, Windsor, Grand-Pré, Port Williams, Starr's Point, Canard, Kentville and Middleton. A signed photo portrait of Princess Louise, Duchess of Connaught, presented to Lieutenant Governor James D. McGregor, remains part of the Crown collection.

Beginning in 1973, biannual gatherings of the governor general and lieutenant governors were held in Ottawa, and in 1995 this gathering of the Canadian vice-regal family became an annual event. In March 1987, under the chairmanship of Lieutenant Governor Alan Abraham, Nova Scotia hosted the second vice-regal conference to take place outside of Ottawa. Nova Scotia was again slated to host the conference in 2003; however,

LADY DALY (1839–1908)

THE DAUGHTER OF SIR EDWARD KENNY, an Irish immigrant, businessman, one-time Mayor of Halifax, Senator and briefly Administrator of the Government of Nova Scotia, Lady Daly came to Government House in the role of consort, having a lifetime of experience in such settings. Married to Sir Malachy Bowes Daly in 1859, the couple would go on to have two daughters, Joanna and Caroline. For many years she served as President of the Ladies' Auxiliary of the Mission to Deep Sea Fisheries and was active in other charitable societies. Along with her sister, Lady Fane, they were well known as amateur actresses, having "won more than local fame for their impersonations at theatricals given at Government House."[70] She was said to have been a supreme hostess during the 1901 Royal Tour of the Duke and Duchess of Cornwall and York (the future King George V and Queen Mary).

ABOVE LEFT: *Lieutenant Governor J.J. Grant addressing the State Dinner*

ABOVE RIGHT: *Lieutenant Governor Alan Abraham and his wife Rose, shortly after welcoming Prince Edward to Nova Scotia in 1987*

MIDDLE LEFT: *Menu, booklet, seating plan etc.*

MIDDLE RIGHT: *Governor General Julie Payette with Lieutenant Governor Arthur LeBlanc, 2018*

BELOW: *Ballroom set up for the State Dinner in honour of the Governor General, Lieutenant Governors and Territorial Commissioners, June 2016*

this had to be cancelled on account of Hurricane Juan. The largest gathering of vice-regal personages to take place at Government House occurred in July 2016, when Lieutenant Governor Brigadier-General J.J. Grant hosted the conference of the governor general, lieutenant governors and territorial commissioners. This gathering of the Canadian vice-regal family included a day sail with the Royal Canadian Navy aboard HMCS *St. John's*, a traditional Mi'kmaq welcome and smudging along with a state dinner in honour of the governor general, lieutenant governors and territorial commissioners. This was followed by formal meetings and discussions which were held at a local hotel.

ABOVE: *Annual Conference of the Governor General, Lieutenant Governors and Territorial Commissioners, accompanied by their Private Secretaries, June 2016*

BELOW: *Official Mi'kmaq welcome for the Conference*

H. Wright Smith.

A. Burr

VERSO: *Former US Vice President Aaron Burr*

SIX

A Place of Dignity and Diplomacy: the Convening Power of the Crown

BEFORE THE PRESENT Government House was constructed, the previous official residence welcomed its first foreign dignitary in 1796, Louis Philippe, Duke of Orleans — the man who would become King of France from 1830 to 1848. Since that first foreign visitor made an official call on the Governor, kings, queens, princes, former presidents, maharajas, prime ministers, high commissioners, ambassadors and countless military officers have made their way to Government House to meet with the Sovereign's representative. Although the achievement of Confederation resulted in the foreign affairs function being delegated to the governor general and ministers in Ottawa, there have remained occasions when the lieutenant governor, on behalf of the province, welcomes Commonwealth and foreign diplomats on official courtesy calls. These interactions invariably seek to enhance trade, educational, cultural, military and/or economic links between Nova Scotia and friendly nations. There have also been a few unique occasions when high diplomacy has been conducted at Government House, most notably the 1995 G7 Summit.

Some of the more unconventional, and sometimes secret, diplomatic exchanges that have taken place at Government House include a visit in 1808 of former US Vice President Aaron Burr, who was at the time in exile, proposed to the Lieutenant Governor Sir George Prevost — who at the time also represented the British Government — an Anglo-American agreement to secure control over Spain's North American colonies, and to set out the case for reconciliation between the young American republic and Britain. This came to naught with the election of James Madison as President later that year and the subsequent deterioration of relations between the two countries that resulted in the outbreak of the War of 1812.

During the War of 1812, Lieutenant Governor Sir John Coape Sherbrooke received in secret Caleb Strong, the Governor of Massachusetts, who sought to make a separate peace for the Federalist New England States, which were not in support of President Madison's war. This again came to naught and the war raged on until 1814.

ABOVE: *Reception to welcome Commonwealth and foreign military personnel participating in the Directorate of Military Training and Cooperation Programme, 2012*

BELOW: *Caribbean Trade Delegation reception in the Drawing Room, 1975*

On a few exceptional occasions Government House has served as a place for the Government of Canada to conduct diplomatic relations at the highest level, where Heads of Government or Foreign Ministers have met to negotiate agreements. The lieutenant governors, having no formal role in international affairs other than to exchange diplomatic niceties, have absented themselves from such deliberations.

In October 1983, US Secretary of State George Shultz and Canada's Secretary of State for External Affairs Allan J. MacEachen held meetings in Halifax to discuss acid rain and Middle East peace. The meetings were originally to take place at the Nova Scotian Hotel, but when it was found that a Soviet fishing trawler was in Halifax Harbour, it was decided to relocate the more sensitive discussions to Government House. Indeed, it was in the Drawing Room where MacEachen and Shultz signed an updated agreement for the cleanup of the Great Lakes.

BELOW: *Courtesy call with Commander-in-Chief of Royal Norwegian Navy, 1953*

10 THE HALIFAX MAIL-STAR — Saturday, November 28, 1953

SOCIETY NEWS

PAYS OFFICIAL VISIT

The Honorable Alistair Fraser, Lieutenant-Governor of Nova Scotia, attended by Lieutenant-Commander K. Birtwhistle, R.C.N. (aide-de-camp), received Vice-Admiral Skule V. Svtorheill, Commander in Chief of the Royal Norwegian Navy, accompanied by Rear Admiral Erling G. Hostvedt, Naval Attache at Ottawa, Thursday afternoon, at Government Hous (Photo by Crosby)

ABOVE: *Group of 7 Leaders in Halifax, 1995*

BELOW: *Courtesy call between Lieutenant Governor J.J. Grant and the Mexican Ambassador, 2016*

The highest profile international event to take place at Government House in recent times was the hosting of the G7 Summit in Halifax in 1995. For this multi-day summit, Lieutenant Governor J.J. Kinley and his wife vacated Government House and gave it over for use by Prime Minister Jean Chrétien, who hosted a number of events and held meetings in the residence. The G7 Summit brought together President Jacques Chirac of France, President Bill Clinton of the United States, Chancellor Helmut Kohl of Germany, Prime Minister Lamberto Dini of Italy, Prime Minister Tomichi Murayama of Japan, Prime Minister John Major of the United Kingdom, President Jacques Santer of the European Commission (forerunner of the European Union) and, as a guest, President Boris Yeltsin of the Russian Federation.

LEFT: *Lieutenant Governor LeBlanc holds a courtesy call with the Ambassador from the People's Republic of China*

RIGHT: *Lieutenant Governor Arthur LeBlanc and Mrs. LeBlanc welcome the former President of Ireland Mary McAleese and her husband Dr. Martin McAleese, 2018*

BELOW: *Lieutenant Governor Arthur LeBlanc welcomes the Chaplain General of the Canadian Armed Forces, Major-General Guy Chapdelain, 2018*

In the fall of 2018, a special reception was held in honour of the G7 Speakers of the various national legislatures. Lieutenant Governor Arthur LeBlanc and Speaker of the House of Commons Geoff Regan co-hosted an outdoor reception in the back garden of Government House.

THE HONOURABLE MYRA A. FREEMAN, CM, ONS, MSM, CD (1947–)

BORN IN SAINT JOHN, New Brunswick, Myra Freeman's professional career commenced as a grade school teacher following graduation from Dalhousie University. Appointed in 2000, she was the first female lieutenant governor of Nova Scotia and the first vice-regal of Jewish descent in Canada's post-Confederation history.

Freeman was active with a number of organizations, notably as a patron of the arts and in recognizing the contributions of those in the teaching profession. Freeman served as an Honorary Captain in the Royal Canadian Navy for more than a decade and remained active with a number of volunteer organizations after leaving office. Following the lead of then Governor General Adrienne Clarkson, Freeman greatly expanded the public outreach role of the lieutenant governor in a more robust manner than had previously been achieved by a lieutenant governor in Nova Scotia, opening up and modernizing public access to Government House and the Office of the Lieutenant Governor.

VERSO: *Garden party tea set*

SEVEN

Welcoming the Public: Events Past and Present

THOUSANDS COME TO Government House annually to participate in a diverse array of events. Whether it be to attend the annual garden party, the New Year's levée, to watch a family member be invested with an honour or be presented with an award, or to attend a reception in honour of one of the volunteer organizations to which the lieutenant governor serves as patron, hundreds of events are organized and presided over by the lieutenant governor on behalf of the Crown and all Nova Scotians.

Each year starts off with the Lieutenant Governor's New Year's Day levée, the origins of which can be traced back to New France and Acadia. Originally this was an occasion for subjects of the Crown to express loyalty and greet the governor on the advent of a new year, but also more practically to lodge complaints about all matters, submit petitions and to take in some of the largess provided by the governor by way of mulled wine or moose-milk along with food. Until late in the Victorian era, the governor had a unique role in that he was the official receiver of complaints, "the Governors ... are the authorities to which Her Majesty's subjects residing in those Colonies should, in the first instance, address themselves."[77] The general logic behind this was that loyal subjects shouldn't be bothering The Queen with their local problems; rather, it was far more efficient to have the governor judge whether or not to bring a complaint to the attention of the proper official, who would look into the matter. As the nature of politics has changed over time, citizens are now much more inclined to raise concerns directly with their Member of Parliament or Member of the Legislature Assembly. Nevertheless, the lieutenant governor continues to receive complaints and petitions which are conveyed to the appropriate person.

At one time, the lieutenant governor hosted levées for a wide variety of events and commemorations. From Sir John Wentworth's time into the early twentieth century, "Levées were held on almost every possible occasion. On New Year's day, on the Birthday of the King, The Queen, Prince Edward, the Regent, on St. George's day, St. Patrick's day, St. Andrew's day, on Coronation day ... it is any wonder with all the festivity

ABOVE: *Lieutenant Governor Mayann Francis hosting the 2012 New Year's Levée*

BELOW: *Young adults performing for the Lieutenant Governor as part of a Christmas party, 1978*

which seems to have characterized every one of the sixteen years Sir John's administration, he [Wentworth] ended by being a poor man."[78]

Nova Scotia was the first jurisdiction in the British Empire to abandon the stiff protocol-driven adherence to precedence at levées, whereby senior dignitaries and politicians would be ushered in from the cold to see the governor each 1 January. Lieutenant Governor Duncan Cameron Fraser, never one for formality and a rather approachable fellow, directed this change and "invidious distinction of the much discussed 'private entrée' into the elect few and any many others" came to an end.[79]

Halifax, along with the other Atlantic Canadian provincial capitals, has a long tradition of New Year's Day levées, which are held by the lieutenant governor, mayor, archbishops and bishops and senior military leaders — all

ABOVE: *Lieutenant Governor Henry Kendall hosting the 1946 New Year's Levée*

BELOW: *Lieutenant Governor Myra Freeman and Larry Freeman hosting the 2002 New Year's Levée*

at staggered times throughout the morning and early afternoon of 1 January. As per custom, the lieutenant governor dons the civil uniform and decorations and is then accompanied by the household staff and cadre of honorary aides-de-camp, who are also attired in their highest order of dress. Guests are admitted via the front door and Gangway, with no precedence accorded to high-ranking officials — Nova Scotia being the first province in Canada to treat all guests equally and the first to welcome women to the levée. They then proceed to shake hands with the lieutenant governor, and in more modern times, this has included having a photo taken. Since the early 2000s alcoholic beverages have been replaced with mulled cider and a variety of sweets, although in the past it was customary for sherry and consommé soup to also be served.

There are other standing events which take place at Government House on an annual basis. Each 1 October, Treaty Day is opened with the raising of the Mi'kmaq Flag on the flag mast in front of Government House, and this is followed by a reception held in honour of Mi'kmaq leaders. Various historical anniversaries are also commemorated on a regular basis.

ETHEL GARNIER, RVM (1931–2017)

A LONG-SERVING HOUSEKEEPER, Ethel Garnier worked at Government House from 1958 until her retirement in the fall of 2006. It was through her employment as part of the vice-regal household that she met her future husband Walter Garnier, who began work at Government House in 1947, holding various positions over the course of his career; chauffeur, caretaker and ultimately custodian. Initially appointed as an under-housekeeper, Mrs. Garnier rose to the position of Head Housekeeper and would, along with her husband Walter, play a central role in the operation of Government House for nearly half a century. Garnier was trained in protocol and organizing events by Mrs. Mary Plow, wife of the 22nd Lieutenant Governor. They had one daughter. The Garniers were the last staff to live in Government House. During the 1994 Royal Tour, Garnier was awarded the Royal Victorian Medal by The Queen, the first Nova Scotian to be so recognized. Over the course of her lifetime she served eleven lieutenant governors.

BELOW: *Garden Party, 1964*

GARDEN PARTY

Beginning in the 1860s, Queen Victoria began holding events at Buckingham Palace that would eventually transform into garden parties. As far back as Queen Victoria's Golden Jubilee in 1887, the lieutenant governor has hosted garden parties, with the event becoming an annual occasion by 1897. These events have traditionally been held in the back garden of Government House, although on rain-days, the state rooms on the main floor are opened up to guests. While the New Year's levée has always been open to the general public, with no formal invitation necessary, this open approach to garden parties at Government House was only adopted in 2000 during the tenure of Myra Freeman. The back garden is decorated with flags and banners and musical entertainment is also provided, often by the Stadacona Band of the Royal Canadian Navy. Tables are set up with finger sandwiches and sweets. Various members of the community, often those involved in the volunteer organizations to which the lieutenant governor serves as patron, are invited to pour tea for guests. Along with the household staff and aides-de-camp, members of the different Cadet organizations, Scouts and Guides also assist with the event.

ABOVE: *Garden Party, 1927*

BELOW: *Lieutenant Governor and Mrs. Gosse welcome the public to the 1977 Garden Party*

ABOVE: *Garden Party, 2013*

BELOW LEFT AND RIGHT:
Garden Party, 2019

BELOW: *An investee points to his newest honour the Sovereign's Medal for Volunteers*

INVESTITURES & AWARD CEREMONIES

Aside from the New Year's Day levée and the annual Garden Party, investitures are another type of event that have been a constant throughout the history of Government House. The Crown is the font of all official honours in Canada, and thus it is natural that, on occasions when it is not possible for the Sovereign or governor general to present worthy citizens with honours, it falls to the lieutenant governor to preside over investitures. For many of those recognized and their families, these are happy occasions that represent recognition of lifetime achievement or long and distinguished service to their fellow citizens. The presentation of honours is the most formal way in which the Crown, on behalf of the nation and the province, can say "thank you" in order to recognize and promote outstanding contributions to our society. The orders, decorations and medals presented are tangible symbols of excellence.

Everything from the Victoria Cross and Order of Canada through to the Order of St. John, RCMP Long Service Medal and Canadian Forces' Decoration have been presented by the lieutenant governor in the Ballroom and Drawing Room over the years.

The most poignant investitures are those where the next of kin of a family member killed in action are presented with a decoration or medal. This became a regular occurrence during the last century. The 1901

ABOVE: *The Victoria Cross*

BELOW: *Private John Croak, VC*

Royal Tour of the Duke and Duchess of Cornwall and York (the future King George V and Queen Mary) included a state dinner at Government House which included the Royal Party along with Prime Minister Sir Wilfrid Laurier, the leader of the opposition (MP for Halifax and future prime minister) Robert Borden, and the Minister of Militia and Defence Sir Frederick William Borden (first cousin to Robert Borden), whose son Captain Harold Borden had recently been killed in action fighting in the Anglo-Boer War. The Duke presented his father with his service medal following the dinner.[80] On 23 November 1918 Lieutenant Governor MacCallum Grant presented the maroon leatherette box containing a Victoria Cross to Mrs. Cecilia Croak of Cape Breton, mother of Private John Croak of the Canadian Expeditionary Force.[81] Born in Newfoundland, Croak's family immigrated to Nova Scotia when he was a young child. Croak joined the CEF in 1915 and was killed in action on 8 August 1918. His citation reads:

> For most conspicuous bravery in attack when having become separated from his section he encountered a machine gun nest, which he bombed and silenced, taking the gun and crew prisoners. Shortly afterwards he was severely wounded, but refused to desist. Having rejoined his platoon, a very strong point, containing several machine guns, was encountered. Private Croak, however, seeing an opportunity, dashed forward alone and was almost immediately followed by the remainder of the platoon in a brilliant charge. He was the first to arrive at the trench line, into which he led his men, capturing three machine guns and bayonetting or capturing the entire garrison. The perseverance and valour of this gallant soldier, who was again severely wounded, and died of his wounds, were an inspiring example to all.[82]

ABOVE: *Investees chat with Mrs. Mary Plow following a 1958 Order of St. John Investiture*

MIDDLE: *Insignia laid out prior to an investiture*

BELOW: *The 1916 Investiture Address of Lieutenant Governor MacKeen, 1916*

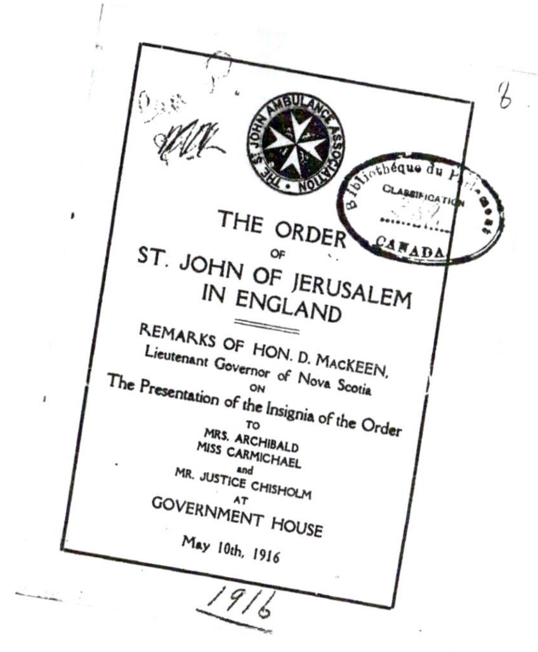

THE ST. JOHN AMBULANCE ASSOCIATION

THE ORDER OF ST. JOHN OF JERUSALEM IN ENGLAND

REMARKS OF HON. D. MacKEEN,
Lieutenant Governor of Nova Scotia
ON
The Presentation of the Insignia of the Order
TO
MRS. ARCHIBALD
MISS CARMICHAEL
and
MR. JUSTICE CHISHOLM
AT
GOVERNMENT HOUSE
May 10th, 1916

St. John Ambulance has been active in Nova Scotia since 1910, and for more than a century successive lieutenant governors have presided over the presentation of the Order of St. John to those who have rendered significant service to St. John Ambulance, such as the teaching and provision of first aid. Indeed, St. John Ambulance in Nova Scotia was established during a meeting of interested citizens at Government House, which was presided over by then Lieutenant Governor Duncan Cameron Fraser who noted "the Order of St. John of Jerusalem is founded upon the principle of self-sacrifice and embodies that essential principle of chivalry — readiness to protect the weak."[83] During one of the early Order of St. John Investitures, Lieutenant Governor David MacKeen invested two women into the Order, Mrs. Edith Jessie Archibald and Miss Caroline Elizabeth Carmichael, in recognition of their contributions to the war effort, along with Justice Joseph Chisholm (who later became Chief Justice of the Province and was knighted), who had served as President of the St. John Ambulance Association since its establishment in Nova Scotia.[84] Since 1946 each lieutenant governor has served as Vice-Prior of the Order, and each year an investiture is held in the Ballroom, usually in May or June.

On a number of occasions the Order of Canada has been presented at Government House. One of the more notable such occasions took place in October 1985 when Frank H. Sobey was invested as an Officer of the Order of Canada by then Lieutenant Governor Alan Abraham, three weeks prior to Mr. Sobey's death. He was the founder of the Sobey's grocery store chain, Empire theatres and the Sobey Foundation.

During the 1994 Royal Tour, The Queen invested the long-serving head housekeeper, Ethel Garnier, with the Royal Victorian Medal (Silver) in the Drawing Room. During her next stay at Government House, in June 2010, The Queen invested the provincial chief of protocol, Florence Sassine, and the lieutenant governor's

LEFT: *Order of Nova Scotia insignia*

RIGHT: *Janet Kitz, being invested with the Meritorious Service Medal by Lieutenant Governor Arthur LeBlanc, 2018*

private secretary, Christopher McCreery, as Members of the Royal Victorian Order.

As part of many vice-regal visits, the governor general often conducts investitures at Government House. The first Canadian-born Governor General, Vincent Massey, held a similar investiture in 1952 when he invested Petty Officer Edward Randall of the Royal Canadian Navy and Sergeant James Parker of the Royal Canadian Army Medical Corps with the British Empire Medal, in recognition of their exemplary service during the Korean War. An earlier posthumous honours presentation took place in 1917, during the Duke of Devonshire's visit, when he presented the family of Lieutenant Eric Dennis with the Military Cross he earned for gallantry during the First World War. As the Chancellor of the Order of Nova Scotia, the lieutenant governor presides over the investiture of new members into the Order. Since its establishment in 2001, a number of Order of Nova Scotia investiture ceremonies have been held in the Ballroom, along with several private

MAJOR-GENERAL THE HONOURABLE EDWARD C. PLOW, CBE, DSO, CD (1904–1988)

THE FIRST LIEUTENANT GOVERNOR of Nova Scotia to be born in the United States since the American Revolution, Plow would come to Canada as a young man and eventually attend the Royal Military College, Kingston. A decorated veteran of the Second World War, Plow went on to command the Eastern Command of the Canadian Army from 1955 to 1958.

As lieutenant governor from 1958 to 1963, Plow is most frequently remembered today as the Governor who established the Lieutenant Governor's Education Medal, which continues to be awarded to the top two grade 11 students in every high school across the province. Plow would also be the first lieutenant governor of Nova Scotia since Confederation to undertake an official international visit, when he participated in a special trade mission to West Germany on behalf of the provincial government. After leaving office he became active in the work of the Killam Trusts and helped to establish the Killam Prizes.

ABOVE: *Officer of the Order of Canada insignia*

BELOW LEFT: *Lieutenant Governor's Education Medal*

BELOW RIGHT: *Lieutenant Governor Myra Freeman presenting the Lieutenant Governor's Education Medal to Allyson Murray and Chad Furey, June 2005*

ONS investitures being held in the Drawing Room. Each year following the Order of Nova Scotia ceremony, the Lieutenant Governor hosts a dinner at Government House in honour of the newly invested members of the order and their families. At this event, special china plates, decorated with the insignia of the Order in gold, are used.

Along with serving as patron of a wide array of organizations, the lieutenant governor confers more than a dozen vice-regal awards which recognize excellence and achievement in a variety of fields. The Lieutenant Governor's Education Medal, established in 1961 by Major-General E.C. Plow during his time as lieutenant governor, is given to two high school students in each secondary school throughout the province. This medal has been conferred by the lieutenant governor at various graduation ceremonies throughout the province and at larger group presentations which are held in the Ballroom. A number of awards for professional achievement are given out by the lieutenant governor at Government House, notably the Lieutenant Governor's Award for Excellence in Architecture, the Lieutenant Governor's Award for Excellence in Public Administration, the Lieutenant Governor's Award for Excellence in Engineering, the Lieutenant Governor's Masterworks Arts Award, the Lieutenant Governor's Community Spirit Award and the Lieutenant Governor's Award for Excellence in Nova Scotia Wines. The adjudication for this latter award is also conducted in the Dining Room by wine experts annually. Accomplished lawyers in the province are

ABOVE: *Recipients of the Lieutenant Governor's Award for Excellence in Nova Scotia Wines, 2017*

BELOW LEFT: *Nova Scotia ice wine*

BELOW RIGHT: *Judging for the Lieutenant Governor's Award for Excellence in Nova Scotia Wines*

ABOVE: *Lieutenant Governor's Award for Excellence in Nova Scotia Wines*

BELOW: *Historical Fashion Show put on as part of the 150th anniversary of Confederation, 2017*

commissioned as Queen's Councillors by the lieutenant governor in an annual ceremony which is held at Government House, normally with the Chief Justice and Attorney General present. Nova Scotia was the first province to gain the right to confer the QC designation following Confederation, and the legal case surrounding the matter helped to confirm the province's right to confer such distinctions.

Following the example set by The Queen, each lieutenant governor takes on a number of different patronages after they assume office. These service and volunteer organizations range from the Red Cross and the Nova Scotia Talent Trust to the Canadian National Institute for the Blind and the Mission to Seafarers. Upwards of seventy different organizations receive vice-regal patronage during the mandate of

ABOVE LEFT: *Lieutenant Governor J.J. Grant reviewing the 78th Highlanders following the Annual Freedom of the City Parade, 2015*

ABOVE RIGHT: *Doors Open Halifax, 2013*

MIDDLE: *50th anniversary of the National Flag of Canada — lowering the Canadian Red Ensign, 2015*

BELOW: *50th anniversary of the National Flag of Canada — raising the Maple Leaf Flag and reading of the Royal Proclamation, 2015*

each lieutenant governor. As a way of recognising the good works undertaken by thousands of volunteers and staff, the lieutenant governor will often host receptions to recognize volunteers and awards ceremonies.

The welcoming of new citizens into the Canadian family is a particularly enjoyable role undertaken by the lieutenant governor. Citizenship swearing-in ceremonies are held regularly in the Ballroom at Government House, with the lieutenant governor presiding over the event and administering the Citizenship Oath. For many new citizens who have come to Canada from countries torn by unrest and political instability, being invited to the home of the representative of the head of state is something that would have been quite improbable in their country of origin.

INSET ABOVE: *VE Day rioters in front of Government House*

INSET BELOW: *VE Day revelers in downtown Halifax just as the riots got underway*

VE DAY RIOT

THE END OF THE SECOND WORLD WAR was a particularly joyous occasion for many Canadians, especially for Halifax, a city that had experienced the war in a more severe manner than any other in Canada. The Battle of the Atlantic was the longest battle of the war and, as the most important port in Canada, Halifax was a frenetic hub of activity from 1939 through to 1945. With troop ships, convoys, the U-Boat threat and endless string of casualties, the end of the war brought a great sense of relief. Victory in Europe (VE Day) came with the unconditional surrender announced on May 7 with a holiday announced for May 8.

The city, in cooperation with the military, knew that the end of the war would result in mass celebrations; therefore, plans for VE Day celebrations commenced in September 1944. It was decided that liquor stores and establishments that served beer and alcohol would be open for only very restricted periods of time, and most theatres and restaurants were closed on May 8. In a city of more than 106,000 citizens, Halifax had 94 city police officers available, while the military provided some supplemental support.

On May 7 most service personnel were given leave, and there was much jubilation along Barrington Street and in the downtown core. Nevertheless, the lack of places to eat and drink meant that sailors, soldiers and air personnel, along with the civilian population, had nowhere to go other than public parks and the streets. Things quickly deteriorated, and from the afternoon of May 7 through to midnight riots broke out. City Hall was attacked, as were Liquor Commission stores, the Oland and Keith's breweries and retails shops. The riot recommenced the following day and, by the end, 2,624 plate glass windows had been smashed, mass looting had taken place and a staggering amount of alcohol and beer was stolen: 6,987 cases of beer; 1,225 cases of wine; 55,392 quarts of liquor; and 30,516 quarts of beer were also stolen from the Keith's brewery.[85] In modern terms, this amounted to more than 165,000 litres of alcohol stolen, or 1.5L of beer, wine and spirits for every man, woman and child in Halifax. Although only a block from where the riot broke out, Government House, which had been festooned with flags and pennants for the celebration, remained unscathed.

The day after the riot concluded, many newspapers across Canada carried a now famous photo of two airmen and one sailor, holding a case of beer stolen from the nearby Keith's brewery, while standing in front of the patriotically decorated Government House. Legend has it that Lieutenant Governor Henry Kendall, along with his former private secretary, Lieutenant Colonel William B. Almon, and a rotating cadre of Aides-de-Camp ensured the official residence was unmolested. Kendall and Almon, both military men and veterans of the First World War, cut somewhat forebidding figures, and this no doubt aided in the defence of Government House.

DIEU ET MON DROIT

EIGHT

The State Rooms: Modest Grandeur

THE MAIN FLOOR of the building is configured with state rooms, those commodious spaces designed for public functions and official entertainment. The layout of the main floor has remained largely unchanged since 1805 with a few minor augmentations, some related to improvements in washroom facilities and others connected to the 2006–09 restoration of Government House, which included the installation of an elevator and the removal of the dumbwaiter that once accessed the kitchen.

It is the state rooms on the main floor with which most visitors are familiar as these are in these spaces that the vast majority of events held at Government House take place, notably in the Ballroom, Drawing Room and Dining Room. The contents and decoration of these rooms have changed through the history of the house; indeed there was a period of time when each new governor would bring with him a selection of his own furniture, artwork, knick-knackery and carpets to kit out the residence. The furnishing of Government Houses throughout the British Empire had occasionally become the topic of debate in various legislatures, from Bengal to Kenya. To this end, the British government provided specific direction on just who should pay for what in an effort to alleviate tension between governors and their legislatures. The Colonial Office noted that the rooms in Government House "which are usually appropriated for the reception of company on public days, will be furnished, at public expense from the revenue of the Colony; subject in those Colonies in which there are Colonial Assemblies, to such regulations, and to the extent and value of such furniture, as the Legislature of the Government may impose."[86] The direction to governors on the furnishing of Government Houses went further to note that "the Treasury consider carpeting to be unnecessary ... except in climates where a considerable degree of cold is experienced."[87] Thankfully for Nova Scotia, there was an exemption given the climate, and carpeting was acquired at public expense.

The house has undergone a number of technological revolutions with the passage of time and the improvement of various services. From its initial construction, the house

ABOVE: *Coal grate*
MIDDLE: *Servants' bell pull*
BELOW: *Natural gas boilers*

was served by running water, which Sir John Wentworth referenced as a measure undertaken to help enhance the fireproof quality of the building. Nevertheless, it would not be until 1942 that modern plumbing would be installed throughout the house.[88] The house was originally heated with wood fed into the twenty-two fireplaces. By the 1830s, this was converted to coal, with the installation of coal grates in each fireplace and a massive coal bunker under the front driveway. Boilers for radiant hot water heat, along with radiators, were installed in 1890. The boilers were fed with coal until the 1950s when they were converted to heating oil, and in 2008, natural gas boilers were installed. The house was originally lit by a combination of candle light and oil lamps. This would be supplemented by coal gas chandeliers which were installed in 1843, and finally electric lighting came in 1901, with the installation of knob and tube wiring that was augmented over the years. Gas continued to be used in some parts of the house, and the five lamp standards atop the wall along Pleasant Street (Barrington Street) remained gas fed mantles until just after the First World War. A system of wires, pulleys and bells to summon servants from the kitchen was installed in 1892, and the Morning Room retains one of the last pieces of evidence of this token of an earlier era: a porcelain and brass pull knob. The first telephone was installed in 1881, and for a time there was even a phone in the Carriage House.

As part of the 2006–09 restoration all the physical plant systems (heating, electric, plumbing) were replaced and upgraded to modern standards. Up to this point there remained portions of the third floor that were served by knob and tube electrical installations. The first computer came to Government House in 1992, and the first lieutenant governor to make use of a computer in her office was Myra Freeman, shortly after her appointment in 2000. It was around this time that the internet was brought in, and the house became fully "wired" following the 2006–09 restoration of the building, followed by the installation of wireless internet in 2016.

BELOW: *Government House in about 1891, you can see the extension on the portico*

GANGWAY/PORTICO

The front portico of Government House, what is today called the Gangway, has endured a number of changes throughout its history. The most profound of these was the conversion of the rear entrance to the main entrance. When Government House was first constructed the front entrance was off Hollis Street, while the servants' entrance was off Pleasant Street (what is today Barrington). During the First World War, owing to some of the unsavory activities that transpired along Hollis Street, which was at the time known for its brothels, the front door was moved to the Pleasant Street side of the house, to prevent visitors from having to travel at night through an area of town that had a certain reputation. Also by the beginning of the twentieth century, Pleasant Street had become a fashionable thoroughfare and main artery of the city.

Originally the front portico was open to the elements, and consisted of four Ionic columns, with a flat roof above. During Lord Dalhousie's tenure as lieutenant governor (1816–20), an enclosed passageway, clad in vertical shiplap wooden siding extending into the driveway was added. The length of this structure varied over time from two to three metres. This remained in place until early in the First World War when the passageway was removed, and the portico was enclosed with addition of sash windows, double exterior doors and a large semi-circular arched window over top, to mimic the Palladian door and window that is set into the façade of the building. The Ionic columns remain partially exposed, leaving the style of the Robert Adam

LEFT: *Lion's head door knocker*

RIGHT: *A close up of the extension on the portico*

entranceway largely intact. This change was made at the same time that the front entrance was moved from Hollis Street to Pleasant Street, which had been renamed Barrington Street by 1917. The inner door along with its brass door rim, latch and knob are original to the house. The door itself is made of mahogany from Belize (formerly British Honduras) and the knocker, also of brass, in the shape of a lion's head, was cast by Niagara Castings (Canada). In tribute to the Navy's contribution to Canada, the knocker replicates the lions' heads worn on a Royal Canadian Navy officer's boat cloak and was installed in 2010.

LIEUTENANT-COMMANDER IAN MCKEE, CD, RCN (1931–)

BORN IN TORONTO, the son of Brigadier Clarence S. McKee, CBE, ED, CD, as a child McKee spent his summers in his mother's home province of Nova Scotia and would eventually make his home here. In 1948, he attended HMCS Royal Roads and would continue serving in the Canadian Armed Forces until 1975 when he retired to start an investment business. During his time in the Royal Canadian Navy he would serve in a number of positions, including as Executive Officer of HMCS *Outremont*.

From 1956 to 1958, McKee served as aide-de-camp to the first Canadian-born Governor General, Vincent Massey. For more than a quarter century, McKee was a familiar figure around Government House, serving as an aide-de-camp to a remarkable six lieutenant governors from 1975 to 2001 and was also involved in ten Royal Tours.

ABOVE: *Lieutenant Governor Mayann Francis and Rear-Admiral Paul Maddison unveiling the plaque dedicating the portico as the "Gangway"*

BELOW: *Gangway plaque*

In 2010, in honour of the centennial of the establishment of the Royal Canadian Navy, it was decided to rededicate the portico as the Gangway, to recognize the special relationship between the Crown and those who have served and continue to serve in the Royal Canadian Navy (RCN). On 4 May 2010 the portico was rededicated as the Gangway by Lieutenant Governor Mayann Francis and Rear-Admiral Paul Maddison, Commander of Maritime Forces Atlantic. A RCN centennial officer's sword was subsequently presented to Government House in honour of the occasion, and this has been placed on display in the Front Foyer.

ABOVE: *Front Foyer from patio doors, the King's and Regimental Colours for the 25th and 85th Battalions Canadian Infantry can be seen on each side*

BELOW: *Front Foyer from the front door*

FRONT FOYER

It is through the Gangway and the Front Foyer that all official guests enter Government House. Each June members of the general public pass through the Foyer to greet the lieutenant governor on their way to the annual Garden Party. The end of the hall is where the main Government House clock stands, with its familiar hourly bell that chimes throughout the day. The Government House Christmas Tree traditionally stands at the end of the Foyer in between the doors which lead to the back garden.

The Foyer displays a quadra-lingual plaque unveiled by Queen Elizabeth II on 28 June 2010 to officially reopen Government House following the 2006–09 restoration of the building. The plaque displays the Royal Cypher and is cast with text in the four principal languages historically spoken in the province, Mi'kmaq, French, Gaelic and English. The walls of the Foyer also display the Sovereign's Plaques, which list all the kings and queens who have reigned over Nova Scotia since 1603, with the names of their various representatives — the governors and lieutenant governors — listed up to the present day.

LEFT: *The Queen and the Duke of Edinburgh with Lieutenant Governor J.J. and Mrs. Kinley, 1994*

RIGHT: *Front Foyer in 1950*

These engraved brass plaques were installed in 2010; an earlier set of granite engraved tablets had been installed in 1901 prior to the 1901 Royal Tour; however, they were removed in 2006 due to their excessive weight and the fact they contained a number of errors in the names and dates of various governors.[89]

Originally the back half of the Foyer, outside the Governor's Study and Morning Room, was divided into a separate ante room, which in a number of accounts of the 1860 Royal Tour was referred to as a Reception Room. The Foyer was opened up to provide free access between the front and back entrances around the time of the 1901 Royal Tour. Today the back half of the Foyer displays the King's and Regimental Colours of the 25th and 85th Battalions Canadian Infantry from the First World War. These most sacred symbols of the antecedents to two of Nova Scotia's most famed regiments, the Nova Scotia Highlanders and the Cape Breton Highlanders, were originally deposited in Government House at the end of the First World War. Then, in 1923, they were placed on display in Province House, and finally they were deposited in the Provincial Archives. In 2016, in honour of the centennial of the 85th Canadian Infantry departing for Europe, and as the Province's main commemoration of the centennial of the First World War, the colours were conserved and relocated back to Government House.

LEFT: *Early Victorian wallpaper which once decorated the Grand Staircase area*

RIGHT: *Grand Staircase, with wallpaper decorations, 1910*

BELOW: *Grand Staircase, 2018*

RECTO: *Grand Staircase, 1952*

GRAND STAIRCASE

What is purported to be the largest unsupported staircase in Atlantic Canada can be found in this thoroughfare of activity in the house. A band of curved steel was worked into the stringer of the staircase early in the twentieth century; prior to this, a small pillar helped carry the weight. With 28 steps, the corners of each tread have a small triangular block of wood; these dust corners were installed in the late Georgian period to aid the maids with their duties. At various points through the history of Government House, the stairs have been carpeted and left bare; similarly, this room once displayed plaster and painted wall decoration which were installed in the 1830s; however, by the late Victorian era, much of the room was covered in heavily decorated wallpaper. Today it has

VERSO: One of the 4 columns which decorate the front of the Ballroom; Ionic pillar details are repeated in the Gangway

been returned to a light painted finish, similar to what was originally on the walls.

Since the reopening of Government House in 2009, this is where portraits of the recent former lieutenant governors are displayed, along with a large portrait of Queen Elizabeth II. Under the staircase is displayed a mahogany hall table and a pair of armorial chairs, carved with the arms of notable Nova Scotian merchant and politician John Leander Starr, a donation from Victoria Hall, which for more than a century had served as a home for elderly ladies.

A coat vestibule is located where a passageway originally provided access to the back of the Governor's Study. Around the time of Confederation this passageway was divided in half and converted into two separate washrooms — or water closets as they were more commonly known — one for the general public immediately outside the Ballroom and a private bathroom off the Governor's Study for the principal resident to use.

BALLROOM

The largest state room in Government House, the Ballroom, sometimes referred to as the Levée Room, has been the centre of official functions since the building was first occupied in 1805. Here levées, investitures, balls, dances, concerts, swearing-in ceremonies, receptions and large state dinners have taken place. Until the late 1920s, the lieutenant governor would host the annual debutantes' ball in this room, and various performances have taken place here over the years, one of the most notable being a small concert given by Portia White, the African-Nova Scotian contralto, in the early 1950s. Since 2012, the Ballroom has been home to a Schimmel grand piano, a gift from patron of the arts Peggy Corkum, in honour of the Queen's Diamond Jubilee.

During both world wars, members of St. John Ambulance Brigade and the Red Cross held bandage

ABOVE: Ballroom, 1950

MIDDLE: A dinner taking place in the Ballroom in the mid 1950s

BELOW: The Queen and Duke of Edinburgh with Prime Minister John Diefenbaker and the Federal Cabinet in the Ballroom shortly after The Queen appointed Major-General Georges Vanier as Governor General

ABOVE: *Ballroom view towards the back of the room*

BELOW: *Ballroom set up for an investiture*

rolling and knitting events in the Ballroom under the patronage of the lieutenant governor's consort. Following the Halifax Explosion, this room as used as a makeshift first aid station by Volunteer Aide Detachment nurses of St. John Ambulance.

One of the most notable state dinners to take place in the Ballroom was held in 1904, in honour of the Earl Grey, who had that very day arrived in Halifax to be sworn in as Canada's governor general. The lavish dinner included the new governor general and his consort; Prime Minister Sir Wilfrid Laurier; leader of the opposition Sir Robert Borden; and many other notable figures of the period. More recent events of note were the 2016 State Dinner in honour of the governor general, lieutenant governors and territorial commissioners, which was hosted by Lieutenant Governor Brigadier-General J.J. Grant during the annual conference of the Canadian vice-regal family. In 2017 a formal ceremony granting a pardon to the late Grand Chief Gabriel Sylliboy took place in the Ballroom with a smudging, Mi'kmaq drummers, speeches and the signing of the formal pardon proclamation.

THE HONOURABLE MAYANN E. FRANCIS, ONS (1946–)

BORN IN WHITNEY PIER, Francis stood out at a young age in one of Canada's most diverse communities of the period. The daughter of immigrants from Cuba and Antigua, she would go on to attend St. Mary's University and later New York University, where she would earn a Master's in Public Administration. After residing in the United States for 16 years, Francis would return to Canada, serving first as the Assistant Deputy Minister of the Women's Directorate in Ontario and then as CEO of the Nova Scotia Human Rights Commission. Francis became only the third person of African descent in Canadian history to be appointed to vice-regal office. The first lieutenant governor to reside in Government House following the monumental 2006–09 restoration of the building, Francis oversaw the opening of the official residence to more people than ever before. Dr. Francis is the first lieutenant governor of Nova Scotia in recent history to publish her memoirs *An Honourable Life*.

ABOVE: *Lieutenant Governor Mayann Francis following the unveiling of the Viola Desmond portrait, November 2010*

BELOW: *Ballroom view towards the front of the room*

GOVERNOR'S STUDY

Successive lieutenant governors have used this room as their office, library and place to review state papers and meet with their private secretary, the clerk of the Executive Council and other officials. From this office Sir George Prevost outlined plans for the defence of the province prior to the War of 1812. It was here that Sir John Harvey conferred with various provincial political leaders to negotiate the details of Responsible Government in 1848. Several lieutenant governors made their office in the Morning Room and gave this room over to their private secretary and clerical staff, the most recent one being J.J. Kinley. However, this has been by far the exception and not the rule.

The desk suite used by the lieutenant governor originally belonged to the Right Honourable Robert L. Stanfield, premier of the province from 1956 to 1967 and then leader of the Progressive Conservative Party from 1967 to 1976. Stanfield's father, Frank, who previously headed up the family underwear business in Truro, served as lieutenant governor for ten months — his tenure being cut drastically short by his untimely death.

The Governor's Study has also served a more mundane, yet functional purpose, during the various state dinners which have taken place in the Ballroom. For these occasions the room is converted into a place for uncorking wine and where the chef and service staff plate food before it is taken to the guests dining in the Ballroom.

ALISTAIR FRASER, MC, QC (1886–1964)

ALISTAIR FRASER WAS THE SON of prominent Liberal Nova Scotia politician Duncan Cameron Fraser, who had served as a federal Member of Parliament, Member of the Nova Scotia Legislative Council, then spent two years as a Justice of the Supreme Court of Nova Scotia and finally served as lieutenant governor from 1906 to 1910. After graduating from Dalhousie Law School, Alistair Fraser practised law in Halifax and would serve as private secretary to the lieutenant governor from 1906 to 1910.

An active member of the Canadian Militia, Fraser would fight in the First World War as a member of the Canadian Expeditionary Force. In recognition of gallantry displayed during the the Battle of Vimy Ridge, he was decorated with the Military Cross and would later act as aide-de-camp to General Sir Arthur Currie, Commander of the Canadian Corps. He lost both his sister and brother during the First World War: Nursing Sister Margaret Fraser, who died when HMHS *Llandovery Castle* was torpedoed by a German U-Boat in June 1918, and his brother Lieutenant James Gibson Laurier Taylor Fraser, who was killed in action in March 1918. Following the war, Fraser served as a lawyer for the Canadian National Railway and rose to become Vice-President of the company.

Unlike his father, Fraser very much enjoyed his role as lieutenant governor, in which he served from 1952 to 1958. Fraser is noted for being the only lieutenant governor in Canadian history to successfully sue the Federal Government while in office — this for granite taken off his property to construct the Canso Causeway, the opening of which he presided over in 1955.

ABOVE: *The Governor's Study*

BELOW: *The Governor's Study in use as a plating station during a formal dinner*

VERSO: *Morning Room wallpaper*

BELOW: *The Morning Room*

MORNING ROOM (CHINESE ROOM)

Perhaps the most well-known room in Government House, the Morning Room is beautifully decorated with lustrous hand-painted Chinese wallpaper dating from the late Victorian era. It is believed that the wallcoverings came from a house in Victoria, British Columbia, and were installed in the 1940s. Hand painted by artisans, the tin wallpaper depicts 86 birds and butterflies along with flora, and it is this wallpaper that has given the Morning Room its alternate designation as the Chinese Room. During the Georgian era, items from China and of Chinese design were in the height of fashion and an overt symbol of affluence. With the original Thomas Chippendale sofa and other furniture and draperies in the Chinoiserie style, this is the most impressive of the state rooms in Government House.

The Morning Room is used for courtesy calls between the lieutenant governor and Commonwealth and foreign diplomats who are on official visits to the province. It is also here that ceremonial meetings between the lieutenant governor and visiting military officials from around the globe take place. With Halifax being home to Canada's most important military base and the Royal Canadian Navy's Atlantic Fleet, there has always been a frequent parade of international military dignitaries through the building. On a regular basis the lieutenant governor meets in private with the premier here.

ABOVE: *Audience between the Prince of Wales and Duchess of Cornwall and Lieutenant Governor and Mrs. Grant, 2014*

BELOW: *The Morning Room*

ABOVE: *The Drawing Room, 1950*

BELOW: *The Drawing Room, during the Victorian era*

DRAWING ROOM

This room is most remembered for being the place where Sir John Harvey, Lieutenant Governor from 1846 to 1852, relieved the last "irresponsible cabinet" of its position and then swore in the first responsible cabinet in the British Empire outside of the United Kingdom and thus helped to usher in Responsible Government, which remains a cornerstone of Canada's democratic system of government. To this day many executive councillors are sworn in by the lieutenant governor in this room. Aside from receptions and diplomatic courtesy calls, the Drawing Room is also used for small investitures and teas. For a period at the turn of the twentieth century, the Drawing Room housed a grand piano and was used for musical performances and salons. In 1936 and 1952, the lieutenant governor presided over accession ceremonies with the premier and chief justice. These

LEFT: *The Drawing Room, 1942*

RIGHT: *Albert, Prince of Wales a few years before his 1860 tour of Canada*

MIDDLE: *The Drawing Room today*

BELOW: *Gilt mantle clock*

solemn occasions took place following the accession of King Edward VIII in 1936, then, following his abdication, the accession of King George VI, and then following his death, the accession of Queen Elizabeth II. At these ceremonies the province's accession proclamation was signed by the lieutenant governor, premier and provincial secretary, and the holders of the senior-most positions in the province swore an oath of allegiance to the new sovereign.

In advance of the 1860 Royal Visit of the Prince of Wales (the future King Edward VII), the province upgraded a number of the rooms and furnishings in Government House. Key amongst the decorative improvements were the addition of gilt window valances displaying the Prince of Wales' feathers and two long gilt French mirrors with marble-topped half-console tables. Following the Royal Tour, the *London Illustrated News* ran a now-famous series of engravings chronicling the Prince's time in North America, and one of the main images was of His Royal Highness standing in the Drawing Room conducting a levée.

BELOW: *The Drawing Room today*

During the 2014 Royal Tour another Prince of Wales, Prince Charles, was sworn into the Queen's Privy Council for Canada by Governor General David Johnston and the Clerk of the Privy Council, Janice Charette. Under the portrait of his grandfather, King George VI, and in front of a Canadian flag, His Royal Highness took his oath and became a member of the Privy Council.

Along with the swearing-in of provincial cabinet ministers, a number of swearing in ceremonies for the King's/Queen's Privy Council for Canada have taken place at Government House. On 18 August 1923, Edward M. Macdonald was sworn in as Minister of National Defence by Governor General Lord Byng of Vimy in the Drawing Room, with Lieutenant Governor McCallum Grant serving as a witness to the event.

The mantle is decorated with a French Empire Style, gilt ormolu clock and candelabrum which also date from the same period as the window valances, although this set came to the Crown collection much later. In the corner of the Drawing Room is displayed a large bust of Queen Elizabeth II which was a gift from the Government of Canada to Government House on the occasion of the Queen's Diamond Jubilee in 2012. The bust was sculpted by Dominion Sculptor Phil White, and rests atop a hardwood base made by carpenters of the provincial Department of Transportation and Infrastructure Renewal.

DINING ROOM

Over more than two centuries this room has witnessed an impressive number of dinners and luncheons involving kings, queens, prime ministers, premiers, dukes, governors general and all manner of dignitaries and guests. The multi-piece Georgian table of Cuban

ABOVE: *Dining Room set for a luncheon in the 1940s*

BELOW: *Dining Room with table set for dinner*

mahogany, with Duncan Phyfe style legs, dates from 1805 and is likely one of the original pieces of furniture to Government House.

The fireplace is adorned with a pair of Wedgwood plaques depicting two British heroes, Sir Isaac Newton and Admiral Lord Nelson. Over the fireplace hangs a portrait by Robin Watt of Queen Elizabeth II in her coronation dress, donated by the Sir James Dunn Foundation in 1958. At various times throughout the history of Government House portraits of Sir John Wentworth and Queen Victoria have hung over the mantle. The end wall displays signed coronation lithograph portraits of King George VI and Queen Elizabeth; the same portraits can be found in Government Houses throughout the Commonwealth. The King and Queen would attend several formal meals in the Dining Room during the 1939 Royal Tour of Canada. Over top of the door which leads into the Drawing Room

ABOVE: *Dining Room as it appeared in 1950*

MIDDLE: *Dinner held in honour of Lord Dalhousie, first official dinner held following reopening of Government House, 2010*

BELOW: *Fireplace and mantle in the Dining Room*

is a plaster painted relief of the Nova Scotia coat of arms, the province's principal symbol of authority. This was installed in advance of the 2010 Royal Tour.

It was in this room that in August 1959, at the end of the first full Royal Tour of Canada since The Queen's coronation, Her Majesty presided over a meeting of the Queen's Privy Council for Canada, along with Prime Minister John Diefenbaker and the federal cabinet. At this meeting The Queen approved the recommendation that Major-General Georges Vanier be appointed to succeed Vincent Massey as governor general. Vanier would become the first French Canadian to hold the post since the French Regime. It was all the more symbolic for this appointment to take place in the province where the French first settled permanently in Canada. In honour of General Vanier, a reproduction Karsh portrait of Georges and Pauline Vanier is displayed on the mantle, and a bronze bust of the General is found in the South corner of the room.

The massive sideboard is decorated with the presentation silver of wine coolers and a coffee urn, which were presented by the province to Sir George Prevost on his departure as lieutenant governor of the Province in 1811. Above the sideboard hangs a large portrait of William Hall during the siege of Lucknow, India, an action for which he was awarded the Victoria Cross in 1857. Hall, a native of Horton Bluff (Lockhartville) and then a sailor in the Royal Navy, was the first Nova Scotian and the first person of African descent in the British Empire to be recognized with the preeminent decoration for valour.

Although Nova Scotia's lieutenant governor has not presided over a meeting of the provincial executive council since 1876, for many years it has been the custom for the lieutenant governor to host an annual meeting of the provincial executive council (cabinet), thereby bringing the premier and ministers of the Crown back to the building where responsible government was

ABOVE LEFT AND BELOW: *Dining Room*

ABOVE RIGHT: *Meeting of the Mi'kmaq Grand Council with the Lieutenant Governor, 2018*

first practised. A similar meeting is held annually with provincial deputy ministers, and in 2018 for the first time the lieutenant governor hosted a gathering of the Grand Council of the Mi'kmaq in the Dining Room. This was the first time that Mi'kmaq leaders had ever held a meeting of their council at Government House, and it was an occasion when the special relationship between the Crown and the Indigenous people of Canada was highlighted by Lieutenant Governor Arthur LeBlanc and Grand Keptin Andrew Denny.

THE HONOURABLE ARTHUR J. LEBLANC, ONS, QC (1943–)

THE FIRST PERSON of Acadian ancestry to serve as the Crown's representative in Nova Scotia for almost 300 years, LeBlanc was installed as lieutenant governor in 2017. Born in West Arichat, the son of a merchant and grandson of one of the first Acadians to serve in the Nova Scotia House of Assembly, LeBlanc's family traces its arrival in the province to 1650.

After completing undergraduate studies at St. Francis Xavier University, LeBlanc undertook a law degree at Dalhousie University. After more than two decades of private practice he was elevated to become a Justice of the Supreme Court of Nova Scotia in 1998, where he would serve until 2017 and his appointment as lieutenant governor. With a focus on the arts, Acadian heritage and physical activity for seniors, LeBlanc and his wife Patsy have travelled throughout the province promoting culture and volunteerism.

ABOVE: *Servants' Staircase from the 3rd floor*

BELOW LEFT: *Servants' Staircase*

BELOW RIGHT: *Luncheon menu cover, 2019*

SERVANTS' STAIRCASE

The Servants' Staircase, sometimes referred to as the Back Stairs, provides access to all of the principal floors of Government House, while a separate smaller staircase leads to the high attic. During the Victorian period, a door was installed to separate access to the lower level of the building, the separateness of the servants' staircase harkening back to a day when the house was very much divided into an upstairs and downstairs mentality. The door was removed as part of the 2006–09 renovations, with the impressive set of 71 stairs returned to its original configuration, providing those peering down from the third floor an interesting view of the house through four floors. In 1960 a chair lift on a rail was installed to assist Governor General Georges Vanier to access the second floor state bedrooms during his various visits to Halifax. Today the principal floors of the building are accessible via the staircase or the elevator which was installed in 2009. In advance of the 2010 Royal Tour, The Queen's Royal Cypher, EIIR, was added to the elevator doors on the main and second floors, while the Lieutenant Governor's Emblem was added to the elevator door on the lower level.

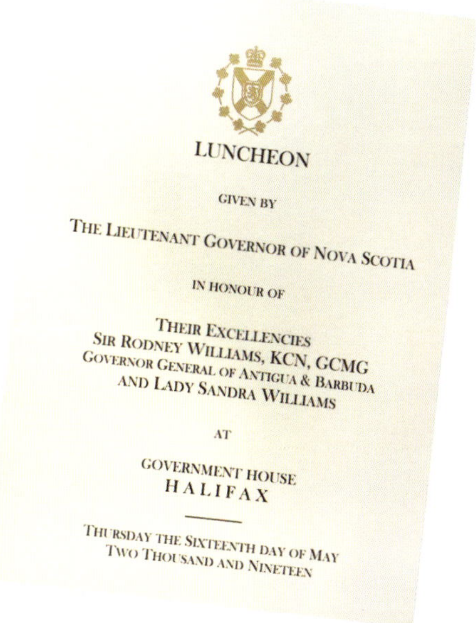

FEU-FIRE

VERSO: *Upper Foyer looking towards the Wentworth Suite*

NINE

The State Bedrooms

FOR MUCH OF THE HISTORY of Government House the various vice-regal residents and their families made use of the entire first and second floors for both official and personal purposes. It was only after the end of the Second World War that the uses of the various rooms became more segregated, with the main floor being reserved for state functions and public events, while the second floor was used by the lieutenant governor and official guests. During full-scale Royal Tours it has become the custom for the lieutenant governor to vacate their private quarters and give them over to the Royal residents for the duration of their stay in Government House. The many Royal and vice-regal visitors are covered in chapter five.

The hallway that leads along the Barrington Street face of the building contains six large sash windows which illuminate the passageways and alcoves during the daytime. Off of this hallway are the three state bedrooms and sitting rooms: the Royal Suite and Saloon, the Wentworth Suite, and the Governor's Private Quarters. Over the history of the house the configuration of this floor underwent a number of significant changes. Much of the floor has been returned to its original configuration, save the addition of three bathrooms, closets, an elevator and the mechanical room.

THE ROYAL SUITE

It should be remembered that when Government House was first constructed it was not imagined that the Sovereign would someday be in residence. Thus, what is today the Royal Suite constitutes a more recent repurposing of a pre-existing set of rooms. The Royal Suite is made up of The Queen's Bedroom, the Dressing Room, bathroom and Saloon. The Dressing Room was originally a bedroom and the adjacent bathroom was originally the Linen Room, where fresh bedclothes and table clothes and other finery were stored. As part of the 2006–09 restoration, the Linen Room was converted into two bathrooms, while the Royal Suite was created from what had been reconfigured as a pair of bathrooms and closets in advance of the 1901 Royal

ABOVE: *The Royal Suite*

BELOW LEFT: *The Saloon, 1948*

BELOW RIGHT: *The Dressing Room*

ABOVE: *Entrance to the Saloon*

MIDDLE: *Saloon in 1942 when it was the Royal Bedroom*

BELOW: *The Saloon today*

Tour of the Duke and Duchess of Cornwall and York (the future King George v and Queen Mary). Originally The Queen's Bedroom was just another bedroom in Government House; however, it was converted into the Royal Suite in advance of the 2010 Royal Tour of Queen Elizabeth II and the Duke of Edinburgh.

The first Royal resident to stay in the suite was Queen Elizabeth II in 2010. Subsequently the Prince of Wales was a resident in 2014.

SALOON

While technically a separate room, the Saloon functionally makes up part of the Royal Suite. The room, the name for which is pronounced "sælün," has been used variously as a sitting room, Royal bedroom and music room. We know this room was once the most important in the house given the presence of an impressive marble chimneypiece with frieze which was carved by the renowned sculptor Sir Richard Westmacott and installed in 1804. The entrance hall leading into the Saloon is located precisely at the middle of the building, and here a large bookcase and bronze bust of Admiral Nelson are on display, along with a number of pieces of Nova Scotian related art.

This room has more access doors than any other in Government House, it being possible to gain entry to the Saloon via four different doors. Richly illuminated during the daytime with three full-length sash windows, one gets an idea of the grandeur in which the Wentworths lived in Government House during their tenure.

Today it has returned to its original purpose as a sitting room, which adjoins the Governor's private quarters and the Royal suite. It was in this room that Joseph Howe laid in state following his death, three weeks after taking office as lieutenant governor, and a small funeral service was held for members of his immediate family. In 1901, the Saloon was converted

BELOW: *The Saloon today*

from a sitting room into the Royal bedroom for the 1901 Royal Tour of the Duke and Duchess of Cornwall and York. The adjoining bedroom, which is now The Queen's Bedroom, was converted into bathrooms and a closet. The room was redecorated in 1951 for the Royal Tour of Princess Elizabeth and Prince Philip, and The Queen stayed here again during the 1994 Royal Tour. With the restoration of Government House, the room was returned to its original purpose, as a sitting room, with The Queen's Bedroom now located in the adjacent room with its dressing room and bathroom located in the south end of the floor.

WENTWORTH SUITE

Legend has it that the wife of a lieutenant governor who used the sitting room as a nursery had the windows on the south side of this room bricked up to prevent an intruder from climbing the drainpipe and snatching her baby. A small built-in china cabinet was installed in one of the former window alcoves early in the history of the house. These were the rooms that Lady Wentworth kept as her private quarters from 1805 to 1808. With a large bedroom and commodious sitting room and fireplace, this comfortable suite often hosts the governor general and other official visitors when they make tours of the province. One notable item on display in the sitting room is a military officer's commission

ABOVE LEFT AND RIGHT:
The Wentworth Sitting Room today

BELOW: *The Wentworth Bedroom*

ABOVE: *The Wentworth Sitting Room setup as a bedroom, 1948*

BELOW: *Officer's Commission issued by Sir John Wentworth*

signed by Sir John Wentworth in 1797, a gift from the family of former Lieutenant Governor Brigadier Victor de B. Oland. As in the Saloon, the ceiling light fixtures are ormolu gilt bronze gasoliers, which have been retrofitted for modern electric lightbulbs. Most likely of French manufacture, these impressive metalworks were installed in Government House in 1850. The fixtures were originally used in the Ballroom but were removed before the conclusion of the Victorian era and placed into storage over the Carriage House and only rediscovered in 2007. They were subsequently placed into use in the state bedrooms as part of the 2006–09 restoration of the building.

GOVERNOR'S PRIVATE QUARTERS

The private quarters, where the lieutenant governor and his or her family reside, take up precisely as much space as the Ballroom, which is immediately below the suite. Prior to the 1947 remodelling of Government House, which included upgrading all of the plumbing and heating systems, the Governor's Private Quarters were divided into three principal rooms: the Governor's Sitting Room, the Governor's Bedroom — to which was attached a modest corner bathroom — and the Consort's Bedroom. Shortly after J.A.D. McCurdy was sworn-in as lieutenant governor, this part of the residence underwent significant changes, with the expansion of the bathroom and sitting room and the inclusion of a dressing room in the area once occupied by the Governor's Bedroom. Today an ample sitting room with its imposing bowed windows faces Barrington Street, while the middle of the suite contains a full kitchen, dressing room and bathroom and, finally, the back half provides a bedroom for the vice-regal couple. Some vice-regal families have occupied the entire second floor. Sir John Wentworth and Lady Wentworth kept separate suites, Sir John in the Governor's Private Quarters and Lady Frances in the Wentworth Suite.

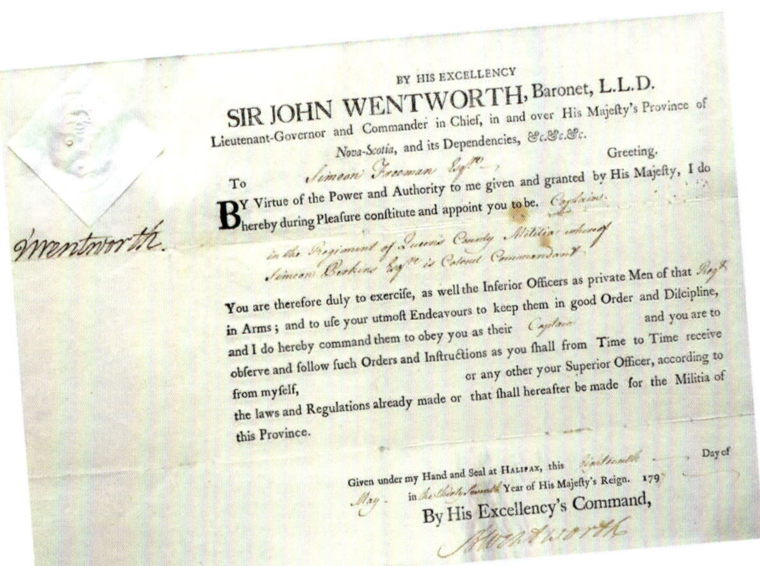

BY HIS EXCELLENCY

SIR JOHN WENTWORTH, Baronet, L.L.D.

Lieutenant-Governor and Commander in Chief, in and over His Majesty's Province of Nova-Scotia, and its Dependencies, &c.&c.&c.

Wentworth.

To Simeon Freeman Esq.re Greeting.

BY Virtue of the Power and Authority to me given and granted by His Majesty, I do hereby during Pleasure constitute and appoint you to be. Captain in the Regiment of Queen's County Militia whereof Simeon Perkins Esq.re is Colonel Commandant

You are therefore duly to exercise, as well the Inferior Officers as private Men of that Regt in Arms; and to use your utmost Endeavours to keep them in good Order and Discipline, and I do hereby command them to obey you as their Captain and you are to observe and follow such Orders and Instructions as you shall from Time to Time receive from myself, or any other your Superior Officer, according to the laws and Regulations already made or that shall hereafter be made for the Militia of this Province.

Given under my Hand and Seal at HALIFAX, this Sixteenth Day of May in the Thirty Seventh Year of His Majesty's Reign. 179

By His Excellency's Command,

J Wentworth

ABOVE: *The Sitting Room in the Lieutenant Governor's suite, 1948*

During MacCallum Grant's time in office from 1916 to 1925, the lieutenant governor's wife, Mrs. Laura Grant, occupied the bedroom which faces Hollis Street and the harbour, while her husband had the adjacent bedroom which is located where the kitchen and dressing room are now situated.

Not unexpectedly for such an old home, a number of notable passings have occurred in the Governor's Private Quarters, notably David MacKeen, Lieutenant Governor from 1915 to 1916, and Frank Stanfield, the textiles magnate who served as Lieutenant Governor from 1930 to 1931.

THE HONOURABLE JOSEPH HOWE, PC (1804–1873)

A FATHER OF CONFEDERATION and one of the greatest and most influential Nova Scotians in Canadian history, Joseph Howe was a journalist, public servant and politician. As a journalist Howe would fight for the freedom of the press after being charged with seditious libel — for which he was acquitted after a marathon six-hour long closing statement to the jury.

In 1836, he was elected to the legislature and helped to lead the charge for responsible government, which would ultimately be achieved in February 1848. Howe was amongst the members of the first responsible cabinet to be commissioned in the British Empire outside of the United Kingdom. In this capacity he played a leading role in Nova Scotia's government, serving in a number of ministerial posts, eventually as premier of the province from 1860 to 1863.

Although not initially in favour of Canadian Confederation, Howe eventually sought to work within the federation and was elected as a Member of Parliament in 1869, being appointed President of the Queen's Privy Council for Canada and later as Secretary of State for the Provinces. This post allowed him to play a part in Manitoba's entry into Confederation.

In 1873, Sir John A. Macdonald advanced Howe's name to the governor general for appointment as Nova Scotia's lieutenant governor, as a reward for his lifetime of service to Canada and the British Empire. Three weeks after being sworn-in, Howe died in the Study at Government House, surrounded by his wife and son. His death brought about an unprecedented public outpouring of grief and a massive state funeral. Howe is memorialized with an imposing bronze statute which stands beside Province House.

VERSO: *Government House c. 1945, Staff Entrance off Bishop Street can be seen on the far right*

TEN

Hidden Places: Upstairs and Down

OUTSIDE OF THE STATE ROOMS located on the main floor, a host of other rooms and spaces are required for the operation of Government House and the office of the lieutenant governor. While the main and second floors of the building have retained their original layout — with the addition of an elevator shaft and bathrooms — the layout of the lower level has been reconfigured to accommodate large public washrooms, boiler room, electrical room, HVAC and sprinkler system rooms. Only the Private Secretary's Office, Administrative Office and Aide-de-Camp & Staff Lounge retain their original layouts, although the use of the space has changed for each.

SERVERY

Originally styled the "Service Hall & Pantry" located on the main floor, this room was reduced in size as a result of an elevator being installed as part of the 2006–09 restoration of the building. It is here that the Government House china, crystal and silverware is stored when it is not in use. It is also here the coffee urns, large tea pots and kettles are set up for use by housekeeping staff during functions. Silver trays, decanters and extra china are stored in cupboards in the corridor outside the Aide-de-Camp and Staff Lounge on the lower level.

Up until the beginning of the 20th century it was the responsibility of each lieutenant governor to kit out Government House with whatever china, silver, crystal and linens they required for personal and official entertaining. From time to time the province would vote an extra allotment of funds to assist in covering off these expenses; however, this was not the norm. Indeed, a number of office holders prior to the Second World War complained about the cost associated with living in Government House and certainly chief amongst these was not only covering some of the cost of official entertaining, but also having to provide dinnerware for upwards of 100 guests.

In advance of the 1901 Royal Tour of the Duke and Duchess of Cornwall and York (the future King George V and Queen Mary), the provincial government

ABOVE, BELOW: *The Servery*

commissioned a set of china for use at the official dinners that were to be held in honour of Their Royal Highnesses. Produced by Royal Doulton, the formal bone china edged with gold and a cobalt blue band was decorated with the provincial coat of arms of the period and topped with a Royal Crown. Ordered from W. Robertson & Son, one of the leading Halifax merchants, the complete suite cost $456.65.[90] It is estimated that one hundred place settings were originally ordered: dinner, soup, salad and side plates, along with tea cups and saucers. Over the years, with regular use, wear, loss and breakage, there was no longer a full set of china available for official functions. Other sets were acquired and gradually substituted. In 2015, a new set of Government House china was commissioned, this time in preparation for the annual conference of the governor general, lieutenant governors and territorial commissioners, which was hosted in June 2016. Made by Narumi China of Japan, the design for the new set was derived from that commissioned for the 1901 Royal Tour and consists of bone china edged with gold and a cobalt blue band, decorated with the vice-regal crest which is topped with a Royal Crown. As in 1901, one hundred place settings were ordered at a total cost of $25,572.14, which was covered by the federal government.

The silver pattern used is known as the *King's Pattern* and features a sea shell motif, popular throughout the reign of King George III. More than twenty different types of cutlery are available for use: everything from bouillon spoons, dinner forks and fish knives to stilton scoops, grape shears and crumb catchers.

The crystal used at Government House is the *Citadel Pattern* handcrafted in Halifax by Nova Scotian Crystal, a firm established in 1996. Procured in 2001, this elegant and locally made product creates a sparkling touch to formal lunches and dinners where it is used.

TOP ROW: *Place setting c. 1850; Plate from the Sir John Harvey dinner service*

MIDDLE ROW: *Plate from the 1901 Royal Tour dinner service; Place setting c. 1901*

BOTTOM ROW: *Place setting c. 2016; Order of Nova Scotia Plate, from the 2016 dinner service*

ABOVE: *Kitchen today*

INSET ABOVE: *Lieutenant Governor Clarence Gosse, Mrs. Gosse and the Household Staff, c. 1978*

INSET BELOW: *The Household Staff following the restoration of Government House, c. 2011*

KITCHEN

The location of the present kitchen was only established as part of the 2006–09 restoration of the building. It is at the heart of the lower level and it is from here that the unavoidably enticing aroma of the Master Chef's creations emanate. From this modest space, a formal five-course meal for upwards of 75 guests, or a Garden Party for 800, can be prepared. Off to the south side of the kitchen is the Chef's office, which serves as both a space for administrative work, an ersatz pantry and a place to store seldom-used pieces of culinary equipment.

THE HOUSEHOLD

SINCE THE WENTWORTHS moved into Government House in 1805, each lieutenant governor has been served by a household staff. Headed by the private secretary, who serves as the lieutenant governor's chief of staff, today the household staff includes housekeepers, a master chef and a chauffeur. There are also the administrative staff who oversee the operation of the lieutenant governor's programme composed of in-house and external events, along with the aides-de-camp who accompany the lieutenant governor to every official event.

The household was originally divided along strict class lines, with the private secretary and aides-de-camp being considered as holders of Crown appointments, while the other staff were considered "servants" in the pejorative sense. The specific occupations of the household staff have changed over the years, depending on the requirements of the lieutenant governor and his consort; the size of the staff also depended in large part upon the financial status of the lieutenant governor, given that until the middle of the twentieth century they were personally responsible to furnish the salaries of the households staff, other than the private secretary. In addition to obvious positions which continue to make up part of the household staff, such as the housekeepers, chef and chauffeur, there have been a myriad of now defunct positions which disappeared as a result of various technological advances and changes. These included charwomen, scullery maids, coal boys, stable boys, footmen, doormen, valets, cooks and fendersmiths.

ABOVE: *Kitchen, 1948*
MIDDLE: *Kitchen today*
BELOW: *Administrative Offices*

ADMINISTRATIVE OFFICE (OLD KITCHEN)

Situated directly below the Dining Room, what is today the Administrative Office of the Office of the Lieutenant Governor was originally the main kitchen for Government House. The massive hearth along the south wall and the bread oven in the corner of the room, the latter of which was reconstructed during the 2006–09 restoration, would have been kept in operation year around. A dumbwaiter was once located in the alcove to allow for easy transport of hot food up to waiting guests in the Dining Room. It was only in 1947 that a modern kitchen with an electric stove and refrigerator (in place of an icebox) was installed. Away from the prying eyes of the Governor and his wife, the original kitchen served as a hub of life for the household staff, with meals provided and a more relaxed atmosphere than on the upper floors.

Today the Administrative Office occupies this space, having been retrofitted to accommodate up to six desks/work stations along with the working files, stationery storage and a photocopier. It is in every sense a modern office set into historical surroundings.

BELOW: *Private Secretary's Office*

AIDE-DE-CAMP & STAFF LOUNGE

This room has had many uses over the years: storage, a staff bedroom, a games room and today it is used as a place for the household staff and aides-de-camp to take meals, relax and socialize. During the 1960s and 1970s the room was outfitted with a ping pong table and naturally became known as the "Ping Pong Room." During the 2006–09 restoration it was decided to retain the modest window which looks into another room. It remains a mystery as to why a window was originally installed in this location.

PRIVATE SECRETARY'S OFFICE

Since the arrival of the French at Port Royal in 1604, each of the Sovereign's representatives in what has become the modern day province of Nova Scotia has been served by a private secretary, who is the chief of staff to the lieutenant governor.

The Private Secretary's Office was used as a scullery and then as servants' quarters for most of the 20th century. The last household staff to reside on site were Walter and Ethel Garnier. Walter served variously as chauffeur and then custodian, while his wife Ethel served as chief housekeeper, the two dedicating a remarkable century of service to Government House. Walter lived in this room from 1947 until he retired in 2006. Following the restoration of Government House between 2006 and 2009 and the appointment of the first full private secretary to take up the post since the end of the Second World War, it was decided to convert the space into the Private Secretary's Office. The impressive mahogany partner's desk had served as the lieutenant governor's desk for many years. The exposed stone and brick, with grey slate flooring, offers the room a cozy if somewhat mediaeval atmosphere.

ABOVE: *High Attic*

BELOW: *Exposed lath and plaster in the high attic*

INSET: *Mrs. F. Audrey Dunphy and her fiancé, Lieutenant Gordon H. Dunphy,* RCNVR

THIRD FLOOR

The layout of the third floor has been augmented slightly to accommodate the installation of a powder room and full bathroom. The remainder is configured with three bedrooms, which are used by the staff of official visitors, a single linen closet — the only one in the entire house — and an office for the lieutenant governor's Communications Advisor.

Off the north and south side of the third floor are located the "low attics" which are used for storage. Interestingly, it is here that, over the years, various members of the household staff have carved their initials, names and dates into the wooden beams and joists. Many of those who worked on the 2006–09 restoration of the house also added their names here for posterity. Household staff have long referred to the north low attic as "the land of forgotten furniture."

HIGH ATTIC

The High Attic is designed like the upturned hull of a ship, the woodwork having been undertaken, following the 1854 roof fire, by local carpenters, many of whom were formerly shipwrights from Her Majesty's Dockyard

F. AUDREY DUNPHY (1921–1973)

BORN IN NEW GLASGOW, Audrey MacDonald would serve as the first female private secretary to the lieutenant governor of Nova Scotia. Having previously worked for the Provincial Secretary's Office after graduating from high school, she would take up her post at Government House in early 1943. It was an exceedingly busy period, the Second World War being at its height and Halifax a hub of Canada's war effort. On 27 November 1943 a wedding ceremony was held at Government House in which MacDonald was married to Lieutenant Gordon Hayward Dunphy, then serving in the Royal Canadian Navy Volunteer Reserve. Dunphy would remain at Government House until 1949 when she left to raise a family. She died in British Columbia in 1973 after a short battle with cancer.

ABOVE: *Lieutenant Governor Myra Freeman and Mr. Larry Freeman thanking long-serving household staff couple Mrs. Ethel Garnier and Mr. Walter Garnier, 2006*

BELOW: *Moat outside Coal Bunker*

RECTO: *Moat outside the Ballroom*

who had seen service in the Royal Navy. There are several rooms in the central part of the attic which were once used as servants' quarters and occasionally as convalescence rooms during various epidemics. For most of the last century these spaces have been used for the storage of files, surplus furniture and crockery.

MOAT & COAL BUNKER

The front façade of Government House is surrounded by a moat, which can be accessed by one of two stone staircases located on each side of the front garden. Surrounded by a cast-iron railing, the moat and staircases are not an obvious feature of the building. At one time the staircases and moat provided an entry point for household staff, who were not permitted to enter the building via the front door. Under the walkway and sunken gardens located in front of Government House is a three-chambered vault known as the coal bunker.

The vaulted ceilings are not unlike the casemates which are a prominent feature of the Halifax Citadel. Two coal chutes, which have since been sealed, are located under the sunken garden, and from here coal was once offloaded and stored in the coal bunker for use during the winter months. Today the coal bunker is an unused space, while the stairs and entrance door which lead from the moat into the lower level of Government House have become known as the Private Secretary's Entrance as it provides the head of the household staff a discrete method to enter the building undetected.

OUTBUILDINGS & THE WALL

The grounds of Government House today contain only one permanent outbuilding, the Carriage House. However, shortly after the Wentworths took up residence in the building, a variety of functional buildings were erected. These included a washhouse, fowl house, outhouses and even a piggery. Some lieutenant governors even kept a cow on the property to provide fresh milk. The maintaining of pigs on the grounds of Government House resulted in a curious parliamentary debate in 1883, which affirmed the right

INSET ABOVE: Aides-de-Camp at 2018 Garden Party

Queen's Diamond Jubilee. The blue and gold sentry boxes, decorated with the Royal Cypher, can be found in front of Government House from May to October.

By the time Sir George Prevost moved into Government House in 1808, the lot was enclosed by a simple wooden fence. Photos reveal that a high stone and masonry wall was added to the Pleasant Street (Barrington Street) side of the lot by the late 1860s, with cast-iron gas lamp standards added to provide street lighting in the evening. Beginning in the spring of 1891, contractors began removing the old fence and wall, and over the course of the next seven months a stone wall with cast-iron castellation along the Pleasant Street side and cast-iron fencing with fleur-de-lys finials along the other three sides was erected. This work was completed by November 1891 at the cost of $4,431.37.

BACK GARDEN

The back patio was once the front drive towards Government House off of Hollis Street, although this was changed roughly around the time Pleasant Street was renamed Barrington Street at the end of the First World War. Over the years the back garden had taken on various forms. Originally a circular driveway lead up towards the entrance doors, which would allow a carriage to be driven up from the street. By the 1850s this became a gravel driveway with shrubs and trees planted in various locations — along with a vegetable garden along the Bishop Street side of the property. During both the First and Second World Wars Victory Gardens were maintained as part of the war effort. The 1950s and 1990s saw the back garden reconfigured several times, with the addition of a flagstone patio in the early 2000s and in

AIDES-DE-CAMP

SINCE THE TIME OF ACADIA, governors and lieutenant governors have been served by military officers known as aides-de-camp. Initially this related to the very direct role that the governor played in the military affairs of the province. As the governor's role became more focussed on civic affairs, the duties of the aide-de-camp became more ceremonial in function.

Today aides-de-camp (AdeC) are appointed by each lieutenant governor on the recommendation of the Canadian Armed Forces, Royal Canadian Mounted Police and a number of the province's municipal police forces. As part of the vice-regal household, AdeCs assist in the planning and execution of events which the lieutenant governor participates in. They accompany the lieutenant governor to all official functions and are most recognizable by the aiguillette which they wear on their uniform from the right shoulder. AdeCs volunteer their time to serve the Crown and the province and normally serve from two to six years in the role. A number of notable Canadians who served as AdeCs have gone on to great achievements, notably General Georges Vanier.

BELOW: *Sentries in front of Government House today*

2016 four lamp standards were added to allow for the use of the area in the evenings and also to increase visibility for security reasons.

In 2010 as part of the Royal Tour The Queen planted a English Oak tree to commemorate her visit. For the sesquicentennial of Confederation in 2017, Lieutenant Governor Arthur LeBlanc, along with Mrs. LeBlanc and the entire household staff, planted a tree to mark the country's 150th birthday. Until 2016 visitors standing in the back garden had an unobstructed view of the harbour, which has since been blocked by the construction of a condominium tower.

FRONT DRIVE

What is today the location of the main entrance, the "Gangway" to Government House and the flag mast was once the backyard of the building. This is where most of the important visitors enter the property and are welcomed by the Lieutenant Governor. The driveway has witnessed military parades, notably one in 1923 where the King's and Regimental Colours for the 25th and 85th Battalions Canadian Infantry were paraded for the last time before the were laid up, and many others as part of welcoming members of the Royal Family and commemorative events such as the 50th anniversary of the adoption of the national flag of Canada in 2015. The fence along Barrington Street has at various times been made of wood, stone, masonry and even rudimentary chain link. Today the half wall has been returned to its original format of stone with an iron castialted top.

In 1978 the Historical Sites and Monuments Board of Canada erected a monument to Sir John Wentworth, and a similar bronze plaque was placed to mark the historical importance of Government House in 1992.

VERSO: *Sir John Wentworth, Bt*

ELEVEN

The Crown Collection

While Government House is simultaneously a residence for The Queen's representative and an administrative office which supports the role of the Crown in the province, it is also a living museum which welcomes upwards of 14,000 visitors annually to various events. Beyond the stone, lath and plaster walls which make up the building, there are the objects which fill the structure, giving it the feeling of not only an official residence, but of a stately English country home, along the lines of what Sir John Wentworth had originally intended.

The Crown Collection comprises all of the significant objects which fill the house. A few of these items, notably the Dining Room table, are most likely original to the house, while other items have been purchased over the years by various Governors or the provincial government. Until shortly after the Second World War, most lieutenant governors brought their own furniture and artwork to augment the items in Government House. This is no longer the case, and all of the furniture and artwork in the building are either part of the Crown Collection or on loan from a Nova Scotia government entity, such as the Art Bank of Nova Scotia or the Art Gallery of Nova Scotia.

Some of the most interesting pieces have been donated by generous members of the public. This chapter highlights a selection of the most significant pieces in the Government House Crown collection — in many ways the treasures of Nova Scotia.

PORTRAIT OF SIR JOHN WENTWORTH, BT

The oldest piece of art in the Crown Collection, the half-length oil painting of Sir John Wentworth, was painted by Robert Field, Nova Scotia's most important artist of the nineteenth century, who was also a noted miniaturist. The portrait depicts Sir John in the formal attire of the period and is adorned with a brass plaque carrying the dedication "His Excellency Sir John Wentworth, Bart. Lieutenant Governor of Nova Scotia, who on the 11th day of September A.D. 1800 laid the foundation stone of this house."

ABOVE, TOP ROW: *King's and Regimental Colours of the 25th Battalion Canadian Infantry*

ABOVE, BOTTOM ROW: *King's and Regimental Colours of the 85th Battalion Canadian Infantry*

BELOW LEFT: *Kings and Regimental Colours of the 25th and 85th Battalions Canadian Infantry departing Government House for Province House, 11 November 1923*

BELOW RIGHT: *Repatriation Ceremony, Lieutenant Governor J.J. Grant speaking, October 2016*

THE KING'S AND REGIMENTAL COLOURS OF THE 25TH AND 85TH BATTALIONS CANADIAN INFANTRY

Flags and standards have been carried into battle ever since armies first waged wars. Colours symbolically represent a unit's achievements in battle and are its proudest possessions. The 25th Battalion (Nova Scotia Rifles) was formed in October 1914 and would distinguish itself in France and Flanders, earning twenty-one battle honours and being given the nicknames "The Fighting 25th" and "The Master Raiders." The 85th Battalion (Nova Scotia Highlanders) were formed in September 1915 and would serve with distinction in France and Flanders, being awarded thirteen battle honours. Like the 25th, the 85th finished the war with several nicknames "The Never Fails" and "The Breed of Manly Men."

Following the end of the First World War and the disbanding of the 25th and 85th Battalions, the Colours for both battalions were deposited in Government House. On Remembrance Day 1923 a ceremony was held in front of Government House whereby the Colours were paraded one last time and deposited in Province House, where they would remain until 1935 when they were relocated to the Provincial Archives. In honour of the centennial of the First World War, the King's and Regimental Colours of the 25th and 85th Battalions were returned to Government House following a formal ceremony involving Lieutenant Governor Brigadier-General J.J. Grant and soldiers from 5th Canadian Division of the Canadian Army.

ABOVE: *Portrait of Her Majesty Queen Elizabeth II*

BELOW: *Portrait of Portia White*

PORTRAIT OF HER MAJESTY QUEEN ELIZABETH II

This attractive and youthful portrait of Queen Elizabeth II wearing her Coronation dress along with the sash and breast star of the Order of the Garter and the King George IV diadem. Donated by the Sir James Dunn Foundation, the portrait commission for this oil on canvas was executed by Robin Watt, MC, a well-respected Canadian artist of the period. The frame is adorned with a sterling silver plaque carrying the dedication "Presented to Government House Halifax, NS, by the Sir James Dunn Foundation, 29 October 1958."

PORTRAIT OF PORTIA WHITE

Born in Truro in 1911, Portia White would go on to become the first black concert singer to reach the highest level of achievement in the classical music world. When the Confederation Centre for the Arts in Charlottetown was inaugurated in 1964, White performed for Queen Elizabeth II and the Duke of Edinburgh. Painted by Hedley Graham James Rainnie, RCA, this emotive portrait of White was donated to the Nova Scotia Talent Trust by Tom Vinci, son of Dr. Ernesto Vinci, Portia White's voice teacher and mentor. The painting was placed on permanent loan to Government House in February 2015.

As the Honorary Chair of the Nova Scotia Talent Trust, the office of the lieutenant governor has had a long association with the Trust that dates back to its establishment in 1944. In 1997 the Trust established the Portia White Prize, which is given out annually to a Nova Scotian artist who has "attained professional status, mastery and recognition in their discipline."

ABOVE: *George IV sofa table*

MIDDLE: *Strathcona quaiche*

BELOW: *TRH The Prince of Wales and Duchess of Cornwall sitting at the George IV sofa table*

STRATHCONA QUAICHE

This massive silver quaiche styled punch bowl was originally presented by Lady Strathcona to Mrs. Elizabeth Fraser, wife of then Lieutenant Governor Duncan Campbell Fraser, following a visit to Government House. The bowl carries the inscription "To Mrs. Duncan C. Fraser, with best regards from Lady Strathcona, 25 February 1909" and bears the sterling hallmarks for Elkington & Company, Glasgow, 1906. Lady Strathcona's husband, Lord Strathcona — the famous Canadian fur trader, founder of the Canadian Pacific Railway, Governor of the Hudson's Bay Company and politician — was at the time of the presentation serving as Canada's High Commissioner to the United Kingdom. The quaiche and ladle were donated to the Crown Collection by Duncan Fraser, QC, grandson of Duncan Campbell Fraser, at a ceremony on 28 February 2006.

GEORGE IV SOFA TABLE

This fine George IV mahogany drop leaf sofa table was made in Halifax, most likely of mahogany from Guyana (what was at the time British Guiana). The ornate cast brass claw feet with casters were made in England. During the 1951 Royal Tour, the table was used by Princess Elizabeth and Prince Philip to sign the Dalhousie University Golden Books. During the 2014 Royal Tour of the Prince of Wales and Duchess of Cornwall, the table was used to sign the Provincial Golden Book during the official welcome ceremony which was held for the Royal Couple at Grand Parade. Donated to the Crown Collection in 2011 by Margot Spafford, the table is used for Executive Council swearing-in ceremonies and Order of Nova Scotia investitures held at Government House.

ABOVE: *Portrait of Henry Poole MacKeen*

BELOW: *The Hon. Henry Pool MacKeen at the original unveiling of his portrait*

PORTRAIT OF HENRY POOLE MACKEEN, SM, CD, QC

Nova Scotia's Lieutenant Governor from 1963–68, Henry Poole MacKeen, is commemorated with this impressive portrait which depicts him wearing Queen's Council Robes with the Dingle Tower in the background. Having served as an officer in the First and Second World Wars, MacKeen would go on to run a successful legal practice and also become one of the first Nova Scotians honoured through the Order of Canada. It was painted by the English-born, Toronto-based artist Brenda Bury, who recalled that it was an "easy project" and ended up being "a totally pleasant job." The portrait was originally commissioned in honour of the silver anniversary of Maritime Air Command by the officers of the RCAF, and it later made its way back into the family. This painting was added to the Crown Collection through a donation from the Moreira family and was unveiled on 18 April 2016.

ABOVE: *Thomas Chippendale sofa*

BELOW: *Bust of General the Right Honourable Georges Vanier*

BUST OF GENERAL THE RIGHT HONOURABLE GEORGES P. VANIER, PC, DSO, MC, CD

This bust stands on display in the Dining Room at Government House, the very same room where Her Majesty The Queen sanctioned his appointment as the first French Canadian governor general during an extraordinary meeting of the Federal Cabinet, which took place at the end of the 1959 Royal Tour. Vanier would make many visits to Government House during his time as governor general. This bust was sculpted in 1973 by Alison F. MacNeil using the Bremen Method of portrait sculpture. This bust came to Government House in 2010 on long-term loan from the Nova Scotia Art Bank.

THOMAS CHIPPENDALE SOFA

The mahogany framed, blue silk damask sofa is perhaps the most notable piece of furniture in the Crown Collection and dates from around 1762. Designed and built by the famed English cabinet maker Thomas Chippendale in the chinoiserie style, which was popular throughout much of the Georgian period, it is believed to have been donated to Government House sometime in the early 20th century and was "rediscovered" in the 1970s by Dr. Marie Elwood, who arranged to have it reconditioned and recovered. For almost a decade the sofa was on loan to Rideau Hall in Ottawa, where it was displayed in the Long Gallery. It returned to Government House in 2001, and since the restoration of the building in 2009, it has been located in the Morning Room/Chinese Room.

BELOW: *Stanfield office suite*

STANFIELD OFFICE SUITE

The drawered and open-fronted desk along with the book cabinet were all used in the office of the Right Honourable Robert L. Stanfield during his time as premier of Nova Scotia, 1956–67. His father, Frank, had served as lieutenant governor from 1930 to 1931. The 1940s style office furniture is made of hardwood (likely birch) and was manufactured in the province. Similar sets were used by Ministers of the Crown and Supreme Court Judges throughout Nova Scotia until the turn of the last century. This set was added to the Crown Collection in October 2009 shortly before the reoccupation of Government House.

ABOVE: *Silver nef*

MIDDLE: *Lieutenant Governor's dispatch box*

BELOW: *Sir Charles Hastings Doyle's dispatch box*

DISPATCH BOXES

The familiar red leather dispatch box bearing the Royal Cypher of Queen Elizabeth II was purchased by Brigadier Victor de B. Oland during his time as lieutenant governor, 1968–73. Manufactured by Barrow, Hepburn & Gale of London, the box was used for the transportation of correspondence and Orders-in-Council up until 2006. The dispatch box of Sir Charles Hastings Doyle, who served as lieutenant governor of Nova Scotia from 1863 to 1865 and then from 1867 to 1873, and additionally as lieutenant governor of New Brunswick in 1867, is engraved with Hastings Doyle's name and crest. Made of varnished hardwood and lined with Moroccan leather, this item was added to the Crown Collection in 2010 after it was found in an online auction in England.

SILVER NEF

One of the most well-known items in the Crown Collection, the Nef is an impressive piece of the silversmith's craft, what some have called an extravagant table ornament. Nefs date to the thirteenth century and grew in their style and complexity over the centuries. The Government House Nef is German in origin and dates from the 1820s/1830s. The Nef was an ostentatious symbol of wealth, meant to impress dinner guests — it being nothing more than a highly decorative salt cellar or method to port spices from one end of a table to another. The ship, with masts, sails and crew — including a band on the quarterdeck — is mounted on four gilt wheels, and could be rolled up and down a dining room table. The Nef was donated to the Crown Collection in 1983 by Mrs. Charles L. Beazley. Government House lore held that the Nef was found in the water off Lunenburg in a chest and salvaged, only to be later used as a backyard toy. This is rather improbable given the Nef's pristine condition and highly ornate construction.

ABOVE: *Portrait of Grand Chief Henri Membertou*

BELOW: *Queen being presented with portrait of Grand Chief Henri Membertou by the Artist*

PORTRAIT OF GRAND CHIEF HENRI MEMBERTOU

This painting of one of the most prominent and revered figures in Nova Scotia's history was undertaken by Alan Syliboy to commemorate the 400th anniversary of Grand Chief Henri Membertou's christening. As part of the anniversary, a traditional Mi'kmaq village was set up on the Halifax Common and Her Majesty The Queen toured the site as part of the 2010 Royal Tour. This portrait was presented to The Queen by Grand Chief Benjamin Sylliboy on behalf of the Mi'kmaq nation and in 2011 was added to the Crown Collection for permanent display in Government House.

ABOVE: *Signature on Westmacott fireplace mantel*

BELOW: *Westmacott fireplace mantle*

WESTMACOTT FIREPLACE MANTLE

Carved by the finest British marble sculptor of the period, Sir Richard Westmacott, the mantle in the Saloon was produced at a cost of £39, 4 shillings 5 ½ pence, plus shipping and insurance. Its formal description is "a Statuary Marble Chimney Piece Sunk panels in a frieze, pilasters carved pateras in blockings, Figures in Tablet & Statuary." It was delivered to Government House in 1804 and would be installed by the end of the year. It is assumed that had the cost overruns to construct and outfit the building not been so significant, more of this style of decorative arts would have been installed throughout Government House.

LEFT: *Tulles table*

RIGHT: *Portrait of Pierre Du Gua (Sieur de Monts)*

TULLES TABLE

An exceedingly rare and fine piece of Canadian Sheraton-style furniture by Halifax cabinetmaker John Tulles, dating from 1815, was donated to the Crown Collection by the estate of collector Reider David Olsen in 2018. The main structure of the table is bird's-eye maple, while the cross-banded top is mahogany. The two drawer configuration consists of a single drawer over a larger deep drawer, faux-fronted to appear as two separate drawers. The tapered legs, typical of the Sheraton style, are string and dot inlaid and terminate in brass caps and casters.

PORTRAIT OF PIERRE DU GUA (SIEUR DE MONTS)

This large impressive painting of the first Governor of Acadia was gifted to the Crown Collection by the Republic of France on the occasion of the 400th anniversary of the arrival of the French in Nova Scotia. Painted by Mathieu Verlier, it was unveiled on 15 August 2004 on the Fête Nationale de l'Acadie by the French Consul General to Moncton in the presence of Lieutenant Governor Myra Freeman.

ABOVE: *Kempt candelabrum*

BELOW: *Prevost presentation silver*

KEMPT CANDELABRUM

The largest piece of silver on display in Government House, the Kempt Candelabrum is a massive and highly decorative piece, festooned with cherubs, oak leaves, lions and bunches of grapes. It was presented to Sir James Kempt by the Town of Halifax upon the conclusion of his time as lieutenant governor. Made of sterling silver and crafted by the celebrated English silversmith firm, Rundle, Bridge and Rundle, the piece carries hallmarks for 1830.

PREVOST PRESENTATION SILVER

Upon his departure of Sir George Prevost as lieutenant governor of Nova Scotia to take up the post of Governor and Commander-in-Chief of British North America, the House of Assembly voted funds to purchase this handsome set of wine coolers and tea urn, engraved with a dedication and Prevost's personal coat of arms and crest. Made of sterling silver by the English silversmith John Roberts & Company, the set is dated 1809. It was found in a London antique store by Brigadier Victor de B. Oland while he was serving as lieutenant governor in 1970, and he donated the set to the Crown Collection that same year.

ABOVE: *McCurdy sitting in a replica of the Silver Dart, 1959*

BELOW: *Bust of Honorary Air Commodore the Honourable J.A.D. McCurdy*

BUST OF HONORARY AIR COMMODORE THE HONOURABLE JAMES ALEXANDER DOUGLAS MCCURDY, MBE

The first man in the British Empire to fly an airplane, a pioneer of Canadian aviation, J.A.D. McCurdy served as Nova Scotia's lieutenant governor from 1947 to 1952. Born in Baddeck, McCurdy established Canada's first aviation school and was active in the Canadian aviation industry throughout his life, most notably during the Second World War when he played a leadership role in aircraft production for all of Canada. The bust was created by noted Canadian portrait artist Christian Corbet, who has undertaken similar studies for members of the Royal Family. It was unveiled by McCurdy's grandson, Gerald Haddon, himself a former honorary Colonel in the RCAF, on 5 August 2016.

VERSO: *Provincial Arms over the threshold leading from the Dining Room into the Drawing Room*

TWELVE

Symbols of Office

QUITE NATURALLY, the role of the Crown's representative in Nova Scotia has become deeply intertwined with Government House, the physical building, much as the role of the Sovereign has come to be intimately associated with Buckingham Palace, usually referred to simply as "the Palace". Going back to the first Governor of Acadia, the Crown has been represented in what is modern-day Nova Scotia by a suite of symbols which has grown with the passage of time. As the level of autonomy and independence of the territory grew, from Crown colony to self-governing province, then to a province within Canadian Confederation with considerable autonomy, the symbols have evolved and changed. Nova Scotia's symbolic growth within the Canadian family has often been at the leading edge of Canada symbolic development, being the first province to have its own official provincial flag and unique Great Seal. The set of symbols examined in this chapter represent the sovereignty of the province, the Crown-in-Right of Nova Scotia, the lieutenant governor and government of the province. Some of the symbols of office are unique to the province, such as the Royal Key, while others are shared with some variations in each province, such as the Privy Seal, Vice-Regal Emblem and Royal Cypher.

PROVINCIAL COAT OF ARMS

Nova Scotia's provincial coat of arms is the oldest coat of arms used in Canada by any government or organization. The arms were granted sometime after 1625; however, the arms had existed before that in connection with the Baronets of Nova Scotia, which had been established as both an honour of the Crown (which entitled the recipient to the title "Sir") and also a land settling scheme devised by Sir William Alexander, the future Earl of Stirling. King James VI of Scotland, who was also King James I of England, had been convinced by Alexander to grant lands in what is modern day Nova Scotia and New Brunswick to create New Scotland and populate it with Scottish farmers. These became known as the Ancient Arms of Nova Scotia, and depict at the centre the Royal shield of Scotland, superimposed on a

LEFT: *Provincial Coat of Arms, 1868–1929*

RIGHT: *Provincial Coat of Arms*

BELOW: *Baronet of Nova Scotia Insignia*

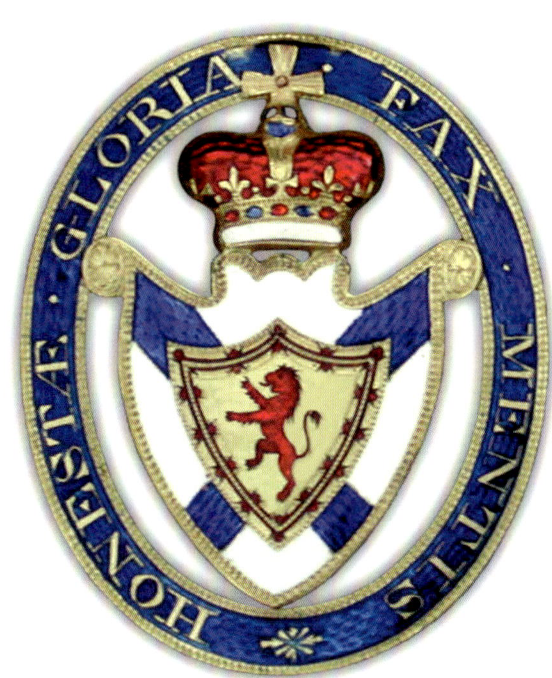

St. Andrew's Cross. In honour of the historic presence of the Mi'kmaq and their role in the history and development of what is today Nova Scotia, a Mi'kmaq warrior (somewhat allegorical in appearance) is depicted as one of the supporters, the other being the unicorn of Scotland, which is found in the Royal Arms of the United Kingdom, the Royal Arms of Scotland and the Royal Arms of Canada. The motto, which appears in Gaelic, translates as "One defends the other conquers."

Following Confederation the ancient arms of Nova Scotia were replaced by a new coat of arms, which depicted a salmon and three thistles, precipitously created by the College of Arms in London in 1868 and assigned to the province by Queen Victoria. This decision would be superseded with the return of the Ancient Arms of Nova Scotia in January 1929 after a number of MLAs lobbied for a return to the more majestic and historical grant of arms.

The shield of the provincial coat of arms is used as the central element in the vice-regal emblem and on

BELOW: *Flag of the Lieutenant Governor flying at Government House*

the Lieutenant Governor's Flag. The arms are a familiar symbol throughout the building. When Government House reopened in 2009 following extensive restoration work, a plaster and wood painted three-dimensional version of the provincial coat of arms was commissioned and installed in the Dining Room shortly before the 2010 Royal Tour of Queen Elizabeth II and the Duke of Edinburgh.

FLAG OF THE LIEUTENANT GOVERNOR

Since the earliest times members of the Royal Family and the heads of noble houses possessed banners which displayed elements from their coats of arms. Today The Queen and other members of the Canadian Royal Family have personal flags which are flown whenever they are on Canadian soil, to denote their presence. The various vice-regals — the governor general and lieutenant governors in the provinces — along with the territorial commissioners also possess their own distinguishing flags, which are flown to denote their presence at a particular location.

The Lieutenant Governor's Flag is flown on the flag mast at Government House whenever the person of the lieutenant governor is in residence. Similarly, when the lieutenant governor is in the official car, on an aircraft (while taxiing after landing) or on a ship, the Lieutenant Governor's Flag is flown to show that the lieutenant governor of Nova Scotia is present.

The pattern of the Lieutenant Governor of Nova Scotia's flag — a Royal Union Flag defaced in the centre by a circlet of green maple leaves and the national or

BELOW: *Flag of the Lieutenant Governor of Nova Scotia, 1869–1929*

provincial shield — was first adopted in 1869 and used, with different shields in the centre, by the governor general of Canada and by all the other provinces. In 1931 a new pattern of governor general's flag was adopted, which displayed on a blue background a gold lion sitting atop a Royal Crown with a scroll bearing the word CANADA below. Beginning in 1981 a revised design was created for the governor general, a blue field with the crest of Canada (a crowned lion holding a maple leaf) in the centre. It was in this same year that a number of provinces adopted a new version of the Lieutenant Governor's Flag, which displays a blue field with an open wreath of ten gold maple leaves surmounted by a Royal Crown, with the provincial shield in the centre.

While the lieutenant governor of Nova Scotia's flag was adopted in 1869, it originally displayed the 1868 version of the provincial shield, and not what would become known as the Ancient Arms of Nova Scotia.[93] By 1929 the Ancient Arms of Nova Scotia had been restored and since that time the Lieutenant Governor's Flag has displayed the familiar shield. Nova Scotia and Quebec are the only Canadian provinces which continue to use earlier patterns of a Lieutenant Governor's Flag.

Flags have been a constant feature at Government House, the early public accounts noting various bills for flag repairs and replacement of Union Jacks in the period when it was Canada's official flag. In 1875, a flagpole was added to the roof of Government House. This flagpole was designed to be raised and retracted from inside the high attic via a large wooden pole and an iron peg, which allowed for the pole to be stowed during windy weather. Part of the mechanism for this flagpole remains; however, an examination of the wood clearly demonstrates the hole in the roof caused occasional water leakage. During the Second World War the large steel flag mast, which can accommodate four flags, was added to the front yard of Government House. From the flag mast various flags are flown: the Flag of the Lieutenant Governor, the National Flag of Canada, the Nova Scotia Provincial Flag and the Royal Union Flag. During specific times of the year and in honour of certain occasions, other flags are flown in place of the Royal Union Flag. August sees the Acadian Flag flown in honour of the *Fête Nationale Acadienne*, October has the Mi'kmaq flag flying to recognize Mi'kmaq Heritage Month and during official courtesy calls the flag of the visiting country is often raised on the flag mast in front of the building.

EMBLEM OF THE LIEUTENANT GOVERNOR (VICE-REGAL EMBLEM)

Granted by the Chief Herald of Canada on 20 June 2007, the vice-regal emblem is the primary symbol of authority of the Office of the Lieutenant Governor of Nova Scotia. The centre of the emblem bears the shield of arms taken from the Nova Scotia provincial arms, which were granted in 1625 by King Charles I. The ten maple leaves symbolize each of Canada's provinces, while the Crown symbolizes the sovereignty of Canada and our Head of State, Her Majesty The Queen, whom the lieutenant governor represents in the province. Similar emblems are used throughout Canada by the other Lieutenant Governors. Prior to 2007, the Office of the Lieutenant Governor used a plain blue Royal Crown as its primary symbol of authority; this continues to be used by a number of governors general throughout the Commonwealth.

ABOVE: *Emblem of the Lieutenant Governor*

BELOW: *Privy Seal of the Lieutenant Governor*

The Vice-Regal Emblem has many uses and is found on letterhead, envelopes, invitations, documents, the lieutenant governor's website, elevator doors at Government House, the Government House porcelain china, the business cards of the household staff, banners and investiture programs.

PRIVY SEAL OF THE LIEUTENANT GOVERNOR

Going back to the first governors of Acadia, the use of a wax seal — and later an embossed seal — has become a preeminent symbol of royal authority in the province. While the Great Seal of the Province of Nova Scotia is used on the most significant documents, such as Proclamations, Commissions appointing members of the executive council, Queen's Councillors and pardons, the Privy Seal of the Lieutenant Governor (commonly referred to as the seal of the lieutenant governor) is used on other documents. This includes Commissions appointing notaries public and honorary aides-de-camp, anniversary certificates and the authentication of government documents. The Privy Seal is always impressed onto a red wafer (label) that is affixed to the document which is being sealed. The current Privy Seal was adopted in 2009 and bears the Emblem of the Office of the Lieutenant Governor of Nova Scotia in the centre and circumscribed by the text "LIEUTENANT GOVERNOR OF THE PROVINCE OF NOVA SCOTIA."

Previous Privy Seals typically bore the cypher (intertwined initials) of the serving lieutenant governor, while earlier versions, dating back to the governors of Acadia, displayed the governor's personal coat of arms. The most recent lieutenant governor to employ their personal coat of arms on the Privy Seal was Brigadier the Honourable Victor de B. Oland who served as lieutenant governor from 1968 to 1973.

ABOVE: *Royal Arms over Ballroom doors*

BELOW: *Royal Arms of Canada*

ROYAL ARMS AND CYPHERS

Throughout Government House are various representations of the Royal Arms which have been used to represent Canada's sovereigns since before Confederation until the proclamation of the Royal Arms in right of Canada by King George V in 1921. Over the doors leading into the Ballroom are hung a gilded early Victorian version of the Royal Arms which were found in the attic of the Carriage House. In the Drawing Room a chromographic painted version of the Royal Arms hangs over the entrance that leads into the Dining Room. The bulkhead at the base of the Servants' Staircase, which leads to the Lower Level of Government House, displays a wooden panel displaying the 1921 version of the Royal Arms of Canada with the cypher E R, from early in The Queen's reign, likely dating from 1954. Over the door jamb which leads from the Servants' Staircase

ABOVE: *Royal Cypher on elevator doors*

BELOW: *Royal Arms clock*

into the Main Foyer is a small gild brass version of the Royal Arms dating from the late Victorian era, with the centre shield removed and replaced with a clock, similar to several clocks that were installed in the central block of Parliament in Ottawa. This particular example was purchased from an auction in Australia and installed in 2010.

The Royal Cypher of Queen Elizabeth II is displayed on the brass elevator doors on the main floor and second floor, as well as a pair of banners which hang in the Ballroom. As the Royal Cypher is the personal symbol of the Sovereign, its use is highly regulated. Even after the demise of the Sovereign, representations of their Royal Cypher remain in place in perpetuity on permanent architectural features, while it is updated on other items such as medals, seals, letterhead and certificates.

BELOW: *Chancellor's Chain of the Order of Nova Scotia*

CHANCELLOR'S CHAIN OF THE ORDER OF NOVA SCOTIA

Established in 2001 by an Act of the Legislature, the Order of Nova Scotia is the highest honour conferred by the Crown in Right of Nova Scotia. Nova Scotia emulated the example set by the Order of Canada, which was created by The Queen in 1967 and which was replicated in all of the other provinces across Canada. The Order consists of a single level, and up to six people are invested into the Order each year.

An independent advisory council receives nominations from the general public annually and recommends to the lieutenant governor who should be appointed to the Order. Members of the Order are invested by the lieutenant governor, who serves as Chancellor of the Order. The insignia of the Order includes a full-size neck badge, a miniature medal (for wear during evening functions) and a lapel badge (for daily wear). Annually an investiture ceremony is held in the Red Chamber at Province House or in the Ballroom at Government House where the lieutenant governor presides over the presentation. This is followed by a dinner which is held in honour of the newest members of the Order.

The insignia of the Order of Nova Scotia incorporates the provincial flower, the mayflower, and the shield from the provincial coat of arms surmounted by a Royal Crown. It was designed by Christopher Cairns from the provincial communications department, with permission to use the Royal Crown having been granted by Her Majesty The Queen.

ABOVE: *Order of Nova Scotia insignia*

BELOW: *Lieutenant Governor Myra Freeman, invested as first Chancellor of the Order of Nova Scotia*

As with many other orders throughout the Commonwealth, it is customary for the various senior officials responsible for the Order to wear a special insignia to denote their office. For the Order of Canada, The Queen, as Head of the Order, wears a special jewel-encrusted Sovereign's Badge, while the governor general, who serves as Chancellor and Principal Companion of the Order, wears a Chancellor's chain of office at investitures and certain other state events.

At the time the Chancellor's Chain of the Order of Nova Scotia was created, only the Saskatchewan Order of Merit and Order of British Columbia had special insignia for their Chancellors. The concept for the chain was devised by Christopher McCreery and the precise detail and design was undertaken by Lieutenant-Colonel Carl Gauthier of the Department of National Defence's Directorate of Honours and Recognition. The design of the chain is based on that of the Order of Canada Chancellor's chain, with the central devise being a shield of the province surmounted by a Royal Crown, and then the various elements of the chain composed of the mayflower insignia of the Order and the Cross of St. Andrew and shield of Scotland — both taken from the provincial flag. A pair of chains were manufactured in gold-plated sterling silver and enamel by Pressed Metal Products of Vancouver, BC, and delivered in late 2014. One chain is on permanent display in the Ballroom, while the other is worn by the lieutenant governor at Order of Nova Scotia investitures and whenever the lieutenant governor is wearing the Civil Uniform, which is traditionally worn for the New Year's Day Levée and Speeches from the Throne.

The Chancellor's Chain was first worn by Brigadier-General the Honourable J.J. Grant at the New Year's Day Levée on 1 January 2015. The presentation of the chain is now also incorporated into the Installation Ceremony for each new lieutenant governor whereby the chain is presented by the Chair of the Order of Nova Scotia Advisory Council to the lieutenant governor on a special investiture pillow shortly after the new lieutenant governor swears the Oath of Allegiance and Oath of Office.

HONORARY AIDE-DE-CAMP CYPHER

Going back to the establishment of the Office of the Governor of the Colony of Nova Scotia, each governor and then lieutenant governor has been served by aides-de-camp, military officers whose role is to assist the governor in their ceremonial duties. Aides-de-camp to the Sovereign are known as Equerries, and when a member of the Canadian Royal Family goes on tour in Canada, a member of the Canadian Armed Forces is appointed as their Equerry for the duration of the visit.

At one time aides-de-camp serving a lieutenant governor were full members of the household staff, paid by the British War Department and later by the Canadian Department of National Defence. However, since the end of the Second World War the positions have been voluntary and hence holders of the post are known as "honorary aides-de-camp." Today more than twenty-five honorary aides-de-camp serve the lieutenant governor, being drawn from the Royal Canadian Navy, Canadian Army, Royal Canadian Air Force, Royal Canadian Mounted Police and a number of the province's municipal police services. Honorary aides-de-camp are recommended to serve by their chain of command and their appointments are published in the *Royal Gazette*. While serving as an honorary aide-de-camp, an individual is permitted to use the postnominals AdeC[94] and to wear the aide-de-camp cypher on their uniform. When an aide-de-camp is "in-waiting" upon the lieutenant governor, they are known as the "Aide-de-Camp-in-Waiting" and they also wear gold aiguillettes (cording) from their right shoulder, denoting that they are serving the lieutenant governor at that time. When an aide-de-camp is "out-of-waiting" they just wear the aide-de-camp cyphers.

The present format of honorary aide-de-camp cypher is believed to have been designed in the late 1940s, although it would not be officially sanctioned for more than fifty years. The design is based upon the Lieutenant Governor's Flag, surmounted by a Royal Crown. The badge was granted by the Chief Herald of Canada on 20 May 2011 and is formally described as: *The Royal Union Badge proper charged with a plate bearing the shield of the Arms of the province of Nova Scotia proper within maple leaves in orle Vert, the whole ensigned by the Royal Crown proper.*[95] The insignia is worn by honorary aides-de-camp on their uniforms to denote their appointment as an AdeC.

THE ROYAL KEY

The Royal Key was presented to Her Majesty Queen Elizabeth II at Government House during the 2010 Royal Tour on 28 June, shortly after the formal unveiling of the quadra-lingual bronze plaque commemorating Government House as the oldest official vice-regal residence in Canada and the completion of the comprehensive restoration of the building. Lieutenant Governor Mayann Francis presented the Royal Key to The Queen at the front door of the building, where it was being held on a gold fringed red velvet pillow by Lieutenant Andrew Graham, CD, RCN, one of the lieutenant governor's aides-de-camp. The key symbolizes the fact that Government House is the Sovereign's home in Nova Scotia as well as the responsibility for custodianship of the building.

The Queen presented the Royal Key back to the lieutenant governor, and it has subsequently been used in the installation ceremony for each new lieutenant governor whereby the outgoing office holder presents the key to the lieutenant governor to symbolize the transfer of responsibility for Government House.

The Royal Key itself is made of gilded sterling silver and was created in the United Kingdom in 1908. It was engraved with the Royal Cypher and the text

BELOW: *Honorary Aide-de-Camp cypher*

Painting to accompany
Letters Patent granting
Armorial Bearings to the
Office of the Lieutenant-Governor
of Nova Scotia
for use by the

Dessin annexé aux
lettres patentes de concession
d'emblèmes héraldiques au
bureau du lieutenant-gouverneur
de la Nouvelle-Écosse
pour l'usage des

HONORARY AIDES-DE-CAMP TO THE
LIEUTENANT-GOVERNOR OF NOVA SCOTIA
AIDES DE CAMP HONORAIRES DU
LIEUTENANT-GOUVERNEUR DE LA NOUVELLE-ÉCOSSE

As entered in
Volume VI, page 50 of the
Public Register of Arms, Flags
and Badges of Canada,
this 20th day of May 2011.

Tel que consigné dans
le volume VI, page 50 du
Registre public des armoiries,
drapeaux et insignes du Canada,
ce 20e jour de mai 2011.

Herald Chancellor	Chief Herald of Canada	Deputy Herald Chancellor
Chancelier d'armes	Héraut d'armes du Canada	Vice-chancelier d'armes

ABOVE: *The Royal Key*

BELOW: *The Queen receiving the Royal Key during the 2010 Royal Tour*

"The Royal Key was presented to Her Majesty Queen Elizabeth II, Queen of Canada, 28 June 2010." The key also bears the text "1800 Government House 2010" indicating the date that the cornerstone of the building was laid and the completion date of the renovation of Canada's oldest official residence. The flange of the key bears the Latin text "Deo Favente" which translates as "God Favour," the same words found scrawled on a piece of paper that was discovered under the cornerstone of Government House during an earlier renovation, and which was referenced by the Reverend Robert Stanser during the cornerstone laying ceremony in September 1800. The highly detailed laser engraving was undertaken by Rideau Lteé of Saint-Laurent, Quebec in May 2010.

ABOVE: *Government House bookplate*

BELOW: *The Queen receiving the Royal Key during the 2010 Royal Tour*

GOVERNMENT HOUSE BOOKPLATE

The Office of the Lieutenant Governor has a modest collection of books which have been acquired by gift or purchase and which comprise the vice-regal library. It has long been custom to denote ownership of books by affixing a bookplate on the inside cover. A number of lieutenant governors have commissioned personal bookplates that incorporate their personal coat of arms. The Government House bookplate was designed and drawn by the renowned heraldic artist Gordon Macpherson, CM, Niagara Herald Extraordinary of the Canadian Heraldic Authority at Rideau Hall. The Government House bookplate incorporates both the Emblem of the Office of the Lieutenant Governor in the centre and the badge of the Order of Nova Scotia along each side.

LEFT: *Vice-Regal Recognition Badge*
MIDDLE: *Vice-Regal Recognition Pin*
RIGHT: *Gold Medal of Government House*

VICE-REGAL RECOGNITION BADGE

Upon the assumption of office, the lieutenant governor is presented with two vice-regal recognition badges. The full-sized insignia is a star-shaped badge measuring 6 centimetres across, made of sterling silver, enamelled in Canada's national colours, red and white, and defaced in the centre by a gold maple leaf surmounted by a Royal Crown. Lieutenant Governors are also presented with a smaller badge that is circular in shape and measures three centimetres in diameter, with red and white enamel and a single gold maple leaf in the centre, surmounted by a Royal Crown. These badges are worn on the left side of a suit, dress or blouse by the lieutenant governor and their partner/spouse at official functions.

The vice-regal recognition badges were established by vice-regal warrant on 27 January 1999, and the first badges were presented on 3 October 1999 by then Governor General Roméo LeBlanc. The first lieutenant governor of Nova Scotia to receive the vice-regal recognition badge was the Honourable J.J. Kinley in 1999. A lieutenant governor's spouse or partner is entitled to wear a similar badge, the main difference being that the maple leaf in the centre is silver in colour. The badge is intended to facilitate the identification of the vice-regal office holder in an era when the wearing of the civil uniform is now rare.

GOLD MEDAL OF GOVERNMENT HOUSE

Created in 2013, the Gold Medal of Government House is awarded by the lieutenant governor for service of a rare and exceptionally high standard that accrues great benefit to the Office of the Lieutenant Governor and/or the Province of Nova Scotia as a whole. The donation of a significant object or item of historical importance may also warrant conferral of the Government House Gold Medal.

The overall concept for this award is based on the Canadian Forces Medallion for Distinguished Service. The design concept was devised by Lieutenant-Colonel Carl Gauthier. The medal itself is 55 mm in diameter, made of gold plated commercial bronze and bearing on the obverse a frontal view of Government House Halifax, circumscribed by the text GOVERNMENT HOUSE HALIFAX; the reverse bears the Vice-Regal emblem of the Lieutenant Governor of Nova Scotia with a blank space below for the engraving of the recipient's full surname, given name and postnominals, along with the year the award is made. The first Gold Medal was presented to Peggy Corkum on 7 July 2013 in recognition of her donation of a Schimmel piano to Government House in 2012, the year of Queen Elizabeth II's Diamond Jubilee.

BELOW: *The Civil Uniform — half dress version worn by Lieutenant Governor Mayann Francis*

THE CIVIL UNIFORM

At one time all those holding Crown offices throughout the Commonwealth were entitled to wear a uniform on specific state occasions, such as the Speech from the Throne, Royal Tours, the swearing-in of the governor general or lieutenant governors as well as audiences with the Sovereign. Nova Scotia has the longest continuous history of wearing the civil uniform in Canada and also likely in the Commonwealth. The uniform helps to differentiate the lieutenant governor from other senior officials and military officers, and in the modern context where business suits are worn for state occasions, makes the officeholder conspicuous as the Sovereign's representative. Duncan Cameron Fraser, who served as lieutenant governor from 1906 to 1910, chose the 1907 New Year's levée as the first occasion to just wear morning dress and not the Civil Uniform, and this resulted in a great deal of negative public comment.[96] Not wanting to break with a tradition that is more than 150 years old, Nova Scotia's female lieutenant governors, Myra Freeman and Mayann Francis, also wore the uniform, albeit with a midnight blue skirt in place of trousers.

Going back to some of the earliest lieutenant governors, it has been custom for the civil uniform to be worn for certain official occasions. Lady Sherbrooke noted in her diary on 11 February 1812, "Sir John went to the House of Assembly, in Full dress suit of dark black with point, ruffles & frill. Star & Ribbon & Court Sword."[97]

The Civil Uniform as it has been worn in Canada came to have three different versions: full-dress, which consisted of a gold embroidered midnight blue tailcoat with gilt buttons, cream/white breeches, white silk

BELOW: *The Civil Uniform — full dress worn by Sir Robert Borden, Prime Minister 1911–20*

BELOW: *The Civil Uniform — half dress version worn by Lieutenant Governor Arthur J. LeBlanc*

ABOVE: *The Civil Uniform — levée dress version worn by Lieutenant Governor J.J. Grant*

BELOW: *Household Staff Pin*

stockings, black patent leather pumps, a court sword and bicorn hat with white ostrich plumes; half-dress, which was the same as the full-dress uniform but worn with midnight blue trousers with a gold wire lacing down the seam of each leg, and black oxford shoes worn in place of the pumps; and the levée dress civil uniform, which was the same as the half-dress uniform except that the tailcoat had much less embroidery on the front — it weighed less and was more comfortable to wear for longer periods of time, such as the New Year's levée. To complicate all this further there were six classes of uniform, determined by the wearer's place in the table of precedence. The governor general and prime minister of Canada, if they were a Member of the Imperial Privy Council, were entitled to wear the highest class uniform, the Privy Councillor Class, while those governors general and prime ministers and chief justices of the Supreme Court who were not member of the Imperial Privy Council were entitled to the First Class civil uniform. Lieutenant governors and members of the Queen's/King's Privy Council for Canada were entitled to wear the Second Class civil uniform; premiers and federal deputy ministers were entitled to the third class uniform, and at the bottom of the chain was the fifth class civil uniform, which is worn by the private

secretary to the lieutenant governor and a number of other more modestly ranked provincial officials.

The civil uniform continues to be worn in a number of Canadian provinces, although Nova Scotia has the longest continuous history of its lieutenant governors wearing the uniform. Today the wearing of the civil uniform is mainly confined to the Speech from the Throne and the New Year's levée, although it has also been worn to the governor general's installation ceremony, when a lieutenant governor presides over investiture ceremonies, attends military parades and to welcome members of the Royal Family at the beginning of a Royal Tour.

APPENDIX ONE

Royal Visitors to Nova Scotia

Relevant details of major events which took place during each visit have been included, however this list does not provide an exhaustive itinerary. Tours almost invariably commence with an official welcome ceremony be it at the point of arrival, Grand Parade or Government House, details of these ceremonies have not been included here.

1786

HRH Prince William Henry, Duke of Clarence (later King William IV): commanding officer HMS *Pegasus*, parade and meeting with Governor at Government House; Halifax, 10 October.

1787

HRH Prince William Henry, Duke of Clarence (later King William IV): commanding officer HMS *Pegasus*, parade and met with Governor and Executive Council at Government House, dinner held in his honour; Halifax, 3 to 14 July.

HRH Prince William Henry, Duke of Clarence (later King William IV): commanding officer HMS *Pegasus*, received address from the House of Assembly, met the Governor and Executive Council at Government House, attended a Golden Ball at the British Coffee House; Halifax, 6 to 7 November.

1788

HRH Prince William Henry, Duke of Clarence (later King William IV): commanding officer HMS *Andromeda*, met by the Governor and Executive Council, late in the visit attended a mock battle on the Halifax Common; Halifax, 17 August to 11 September.

1789

HRH Prince William Henry, Duke of Clarence (later King William IV): Halifax, November.

1791–1800

HRH Prince Edward, Duke of Kent (father of Queen Victoria): an extended stay in Nova Scotia, partly as Commander-in-Chief of British North America.

1860

HRH Prince Albert Edward, Prince of Wales (later King Edward VII): levée and dinner at Government House, ball at Province House, presentation of gifts by Mi'kmaq and civic leaders; Halifax, Windsor, Truro and Pictou, 30 July to 6 August.

1861

HRH Prince Alfred, Duke of Edinburgh (son of Queen Victoria): midshipman aboard HMS *St. George*, presided over Queen's birthday parade and reviewed troops; Halifax, 22 to 24 May.

1869

HRH Prince Arthur (son of Queen Victoria, later Duke of Connaught): visit to military installations; Halifax, 22 August to 1 September.

1878

HRH Prince Alfred, Duke of Edinburgh (son of Queen Victoria): visit in connection with his service in the Royal Navy and to attend the installation of the governor general; Halifax, 21 to 27 November.

HRH Princess Louise (daughter of Queen Victoria) & John Campbell, Marquis of Lorne: installation of the Marquis as Governor General of Canada at Province House; Halifax, 25 to 27 November.

1880

HRH Princess Louise (daughter of Queen Victoria) and Marquis of Lorne: vice-regal visit as governor general; Halifax, 26 January.

1882

The Marquis of Lorne: vice-regal visit as governor general; Halifax, 21 January.

1883

HRH Prince George of Wales (later King George V): officer on HMS *Bacchante*, attended concert in his honour in the Public Gardens, dinner at Government House; Halifax, 15 May and 1 August.

1884

HRH Prince George of Wales (later King George V): officer on HMS *Canada*, hunting and fishing trip; Kentville and Annapolis Royal, June.

1890

HRH Prince George of Wales (later King George V): as Commanding Officer of HMS *Thrush*, attended a supper party at Maplewood hosted by Sir John Ross. The Prince and some officers held a small dance at HM Dockyard and Sir John Ross also held a large ball at Bellevue in honour of the Prince; Halifax, 1 and 24 August.

1891

HRH Prince George of Wales (later King George V): as Commanding Officer of HMS *Thrush*, based out of Halifax; June.

1901

The Duke & Duchess of Cornwall and York (later King George V and Queen Mary): arrived on HMS *Ophir* as part of the Empire-wide Royal Tour, laid cornerstone of Anglo-Boer War Memorial, presentation of Colours to the Princess Louise Fusiliers, medals investiture, dinner at Government House and reception at Province House; Amherst and Halifax, 19 to 21 October.

1906

HRH Prince Arthur of Connaught: visit to Royal Artillery Park; Halifax, 28 to 29 April.

1911

HRH Princess Patricia of Connaught; Halifax.

1912

HRH Prince Arthur, Duke of Connaught with HRH Princess Louise, Duchess of Connaught and HRH Princess Patricia: opening of Sir Sanford Fleming Park (Dingle Tower) memorial in Halifax; Digby, Windsor, Wolfville, Grand-Pré, Port Williams, Starr's Point, Canard, Kentville and Middleton, 1 to 17 August.

1913

HRH Prince Arthur, Duke of Connaught with HRH Princess Louise, Duchess of Connaught and HRH Princess Patricia: depart Canada on the RMS *Empress of Britain*; Halifax, 22 March.

1913

HRH Prince Albert (later King George VI): officer on HMS *Cumberland:* drove through the streets of Halifax and attended an "at home" and dance at Government House; Halifax, 24 May.

1918

HRH Prince Arthur of Connaught (son of the Duke of Connaught): journey from Japan aboard IJN *Kirishima*, toured across Canada, visit to local military hospitals, presentation of gallantry medals; Halifax, 24 to 25 August.

1919

HRH Prince Edward, Prince of Wales (later King Edward VIII and then Duke of Windsor): arrives on HMS *Dragon,* victory tour of Canada, review of troops, presentation of gallantry medals; Halifax, 17 to 18 August.

HRH Prince Edward, Prince of Wales (later King Edward VIII): return to Halifax aboard HMS *Renown* after visit to the United States, farewell visit to city, review of rebuilt HM Dockyard, review of troops at Citadel, visit to nuns at Convent of the Sacred Heart, tour of Dalhousie University, laid new cornerstone for city clocktower, visit to Children's Hospital and School for the Blind, ball at Government House; Halifax, 25 to 26 November.

1939

TMs King George VI & Queen Elizabeth: reception at Province House, meetings at Government House, luncheon at Nova Scotian Hotel, first visit by a reigning Sovereign; Pictou, Halifax, 14 June.

1940

Earl of Athlone, as governor general, & HRH Princess Alice, Countess of Athlone: vice-regal visit and wartime morale tour; Halifax, 20 June.

1941

HRH Prince George, Duke of Kent: first member of the Royal Family to fly transatlantic, review of the newly formed Kent Regiment and the Essex Scottish Regiment in Halifax, visit to RCAF Stations; Debert, Sydney, Halifax and Dartmouth; July–August.

HRH Prince Philip (later Duke of Edinburgh) as midshipman in Royal Navy: visits Halifax on shore leave and escorts Canadian troops to Europe during Second World War.

1944

Earl of Athlone as governor general & HRH Princess Alice, Countess of Athlone: visit to various military installations, review of sailors and troops; Halifax, 24 September.

1945
Earl of Athlone as governor general & HRH Princess Alice, Countess of Athlone: returning from the United Kingdom on the ship, RMS *Queen Elizabeth*; 19 November.

1951
HRH Princess Elizabeth (later Queen Elizabeth II) with HRH the Duke of Edinburgh: visit to Province House, events at Government House, review of RCN Sailors, visit of steel mill in Sydney; Halifax, Dartmouth and Sydney, 7 to 8 November.

1954
HRH Princess Marina, Duchess of Kent and her daughter Princess Alexandra: visit to RCN installations and local hospitals; Halifax and Dartmouth, 2 to 4 September.

1958
HRH Princess Margaret: private tour of province; Digby, Halifax, Yarmouth, Church Point, Annapolis Royal, Middleton, Kentville and Windsor, 11 to 12 August.

HRH Prince Philip, Duke of Edinburgh: to visit victims of the mining disaster and emergency services personnel; Springhill, 31 October.

1959
HM Queen Elizabeth II and HRH Prince Philip, Duke of Edinburgh: presentation of new colours to the Royal Canadian Navy, concert on Garrison Grounds, visit to Camp Hill Hospital, Queen presides over meeting of the Queen's Privy Council for Canada at Government House, formal dinner at Nova Scotian Hotel; Trenton, New Glasgow, Sydney, Dartmouth, Halifax, 31 July to 1 August

1967
HM Queen Elizabeth The Queen Mother for Canada Centennial Celebrations: to receive an honorary degree from Dalhousie University and in connection with the Centennial of Confederation; Halifax, 14 to 17 July.

1973
HRH Princess Alexandra and the Hon. Angus Ogilvy: visit to IWK Children's Hospital, HMC Dockyard, West Pictou District High School, attend celebrations marking the arrival of the ship *Hector* with the first Scottish settlers; Halifax, Pictou and Chester, 19 to 23 July.

HRH Prince Charles, Prince of Wales: personal visit as an officer aboard HMS *Minerava*; Halifax harbour and coastal waters off Nova Scotia.

1975
HRH Prince Charles, Prince of Wales: personal visit as an officer aboard HMS *Hermes*, Halifax harbour and coastal waters off Nova Scotia; ~ 3 weeks, 2 May to 5 June.

1976
HM Queen Elizabeth II, HRH Prince Philip, Duke of Edinburgh and HRH Prince Andrew: visit following Montreal Olympics, arrive on HMY *Britannia*, visit to Northwood Centre, Olympic Folk Show at Saint Mary's University, visits to CFB Shearwater and CFB Greenwood, attend Tafi Royal Festival Picnic, opening of Hants County Hospital; Halifax and Windsor, 13 to 15 July.

1978
HRH Prince Philip, Duke of Edinburgh: refueling stopover; Halifax, 9 October.

1979
HM Queen Elizabeth The Queen Mother: presentation of Colour to Maritime Command (later Royal Canadian Navy), opening of the International Gathering of the Clans and Nova Scotia International Tattoo; Halifax, 26 to 29 June.

1980
HRH Prince Philip, Duke of Edinburgh: stopover from visit to Bermuda; Halifax, 11 October.

1983
HRH Prince Charles, Prince of Wales and HRH Diana, the Princess of Wales: 200th Anniversary of United Empire Loyalists, commissioning of Fleet Maintenance Facility *Cape Scott*. HMY *Britannia* anchored in Halifax harbour; Halifax, Lunenburg and Shelburne, 14 to 16 June.

1984
HRH Prince Michael of Kent: commemoration of the 75th anniversary of the first powered flight in the British Empire, dinner at Nova Scotian Hotel, visit to Coast Guard College, Halifax, Sydney, Louisbourg and Baddeck, 22 to 24 February.

1985
HRH Prince Andrew: Opening of the Nova Scotia International Tattoo; Halifax, Digby, Annapolis Royal, North Sydney, Halifax, Truro, Dartmouth, 26 to 29 June.

1987
HRH Prince Edward: Opening of the Nova Scotia International Tattoo and the International Gathering of the Clans; Sambro and Halifax, 25 June to 2 July.

1988
HRH Princess Anne, the Princess Royal and Captain Mark Phillips: private visit on return from Calgary Olympics; Halifax, February.

HRH Princess Margaret, Countess of Snowdon: unveiling of Shelburne Memorial, presentation of Colours to Princess Louise Fusiliers, visit to Canning for 75th Anniversary of Nova Scotia's Women's Institute; Shelburne and Halifax, 5 to 12 July.

1989
HRH Prince Philip, Duke of Edinburgh: presentation of Duke of Edinburgh's Award and dinner at Government House; Halifax, 21 March.

1990
HRH Prince Richard, Duke of Gloucester: Order of St. John and St. John Ambulance events; Halifax, 7 to 10 May.

1991
HRH Princess Anne, the Princess Royal: attend Nova Scotia International Tattoo, Gathering of the Clans and visit to the IWK Children's Hospital, Maritime Command Headquarters, Mission to Seamen, the Black Community Centre, Hector Heritage Quay and the Pictou Lobster Fishermans Carnival; Halifax, Dartmouth and Pictou, 4 to 6 July.

1992
HRH Prince Philip, Duke of Edinburgh: stopover; Halifax, 25 March.

1993
HRH Prince Edward: presentation of Duke of Edinburgh's Awards; Halifax, 14 April.

HRH Prince Andrew, Duke of York: visit to Maritime Command, dinner at Government House and tour of HMCS *Sackville*; Halifax, 23 September.

1994
HM Queen Elizabeth II and HRH Prince Philip, Duke of Edinburgh: commemoration of 175th anniversary of Province House, opening of the QEII Hospital, Prince Philip tours renovations of St. George's Round Church, visit to the Fortress of Louisburg; Halifax, Dartmouth, Louisburg and Sydney, 13 to 15 August.

1997
HRH Prince Philip, Duke of Edinburgh: World Wildlife Fund luncheon; Halifax, 21 March.

2000
TRH Prince Edward, Earl of Wessex & Sophie, the Countess of Wessex: visit to Pier 21 Museum of Immigration and presentation of Duke of Edinburgh's Awards, luncheon at Government House; Halifax, 18 July.

2002
HRH Prince Michael of Kent: Queen's Golden Jubilee celebrations, dinner at Government House; Halifax, 22 to 24 March.

2005
HRH Prince Edward, Earl of Wessex: presentation of Duke of Edinburgh's Awards, tour of the Tim Horton Children's Camp in Tatamagouche; Fox Harbour and Tatamagouche, 3 June.

2007
HRH Prince Edward, Earl of Wessex: presentation of Duke of Edinburgh's Awards; Halifax, 14 October.

2009
HRH Prince Andrew, Duke of York: Trooping the Colour, Princess Louise Fusiliers; Halifax, 23 April.

2010
HM Queen Elizabeth II and HRH Prince Philip, Duke of Edinburgh: commemoration of the 400th anniversary of the baptism of Grand Chief Henri Membertou, to preside over the Halifax International Fleet Review and centennial of the Royal Canadian Navy and rededication of Government House following restoration; Halifax, 28 to 30 June.

2014
TRH Prince Charles, Prince of Wales and Camilla, the Duchess of Cornwall: Prince of Wales sworn into the Queen's Privy Council for Canada, visit to Military Families Resource Centre, tree planting at Public Gardens, Her Royal Highness visits Northbrook Community Centre, tour of Seaport Farmers' Market and Canadian Museum of Immigration at Pier 21, tour of Hector Heritage Quay; Halifax, Dartmouth and Pictou, 17 to 19 May.

2015
HRH Prince Edward, Earl of Wessex: presentation of Duke of Edinburgh's Awards and visit to IWK Children's Hospital; Halifax, 2 to 3 November.

2019
HRH Prince Andrew, Duke of York: 150th anniversary of the Princess Louise Fusiliers; Halifax, 23–24 May.

APPENDIX TWO

Lieutenant Governors of Nova Scotia Who Have Resided in Government House

The brass Sovereigns' Plaques that grace the walls of the Front Foyer carry the names and dates of service of all the Sovereigns who have reigned over Nova Scotia, as well as their representatives, the governors, lieutenant governors and administrators who have represented them since the arrival of the French in 1604. This list commences with the first lieutenant governor to live in Government House, Sir John Wentworth.

1792–1808	Sir John Wentworth, BT
1808–11 *†	Lieutenant General Sir George Prevost, BT
1811–16 †	Lieutenant General Sir John Coape Sherbrooke, GCB
1816–20 †	The Right Honourable Earl of Dalhousie, GCB
1820–28 †	General Sir James Kempt, GCB, GCH
1828–34	General Sir Peregrine Maitland, GCB
1834–40	Major General Sir Colin Campbell, KCB
1840–46	The Right Honourable Viscount Falkland, GCH, PC
1846–52	Lieutenant General Sir John Harvey, KCB, KCH, Kt
1852–58	General Sir John Gaspard Le Marchant, GCMG, KCB, Kt
1858–63	The Right Honourable Earl of Mulgrave, GCB, GCMG, PC
1864–65	Sir Richard Graves MacDonnell, KCMG, CB
1865–67 *	General the Honourable Sir William Fenwick Williams, BT, GCB
1867–73	Lieutenant General the Honourable Sir Charles Hastings Doyle, KCMG
1873	The Honourable Joseph Howe, PC
1873–83	The Honourable Sir Adams George Archibald, PC, KCMG, QC
1883–88	The Honourable Matthew Henry Richey, QC
1888–90	The Honourable Archibald Woodbury McLelan, PC
1890–1900	The Honourable Sir Malachy Bowes Daly, PC, KCMG, QC

1900–06	The Honourable Alfred Gilpin Jones, PC
1906–10	The Honourable Duncan Cameron Fraser, KC
1910–15	The Honourable James Drummond McGregor
1915–16	The Honourable David MacKeen
1916–25	The Honourable MacCallum Grant
1925	The Honourable James Robson Douglas
1925–30	The Honourable James Cranswick Tory
1930–31	The Honourable Frank Thomas Stanfield
1931–37	The Honourable Walter Harold Covert, KC
1937–40	The Honourable Robert Irwin
1940–42	The Honourable Frederick Francis Mathers, KC
1942–47	Lieutenant Colonel the Honourable Henry Ernest Kendall, MD
1947–52	The Honourable John Alexander Douglas McCurdy, MBE
1952–58	The Honourable Alistair Fraser, MC, QC
1958–63	Major General the Honourable Edward Chester Plow, CBE, DSO, CD
1963–68	The Honourable Henry Poole MacKeen, SM, CD, QC
1968–73	Brigadier the Honourable Victor de Bedia Oland, OC, ED, CD
1973–78	The Honourable Clarence Lloyd Gosse, OC, MD
1978–84	The Honourable John Elvin Shaffner
1984–89	Lieutenant Colonel the Honourable Alan R. Abraham, CM, ONS, CD
1989–94	The Honourable Lloyd Roseville Crouse, PC, ONS
1994–2000	The Honourable John James Kinley, ONS, CD
2000–06	The Honourable Myra Ava Freeman, CM, ONS, MSM, CD
2006–11	The Honourable Mayann Elizabeth Francis, ONS
2012–17	Brigadier-General the Honourable John James Grant, CM, CMM, ONS, CD
2017–	The Honourable Arthur J. LeBlanc, ONS, QC

* Also Commander-in-Chief of British North America

† Would become Governor-in-Chief of British North America

APPENDIX THREE

Private Secretaries to the Lieutenant Governor Since Confederation

When Pierre Du Gua de Monts arrived at Port Royal in 1604, he was accompanied by his secretary, Jean Ralluau. Since that time, the Sovereign's representatives in what would become Nova Scotia, the various governors and lieutenant governors, have been served by a private secretary. While the position of governor is the oldest state office in Canada, the post of private secretary became the first civil service job. In Nova Scotia from 1964 to 2009 the job-title "executive assistant" was used in place of "private secretary."

1867–73	Mr. Harry Moody *
1873	Mr. William Howe
1873–74	Captain Samuel Adams **
1874–77	Lieutenant John Hicks, RN
1877–1900	Lieutenant-Colonel Holt Waring Clerke
1900–07	Lieutenant-Colonel Guy Carleton Jones, MD †
1907–10	Mr. Alistair Fraser ‡
1911–23	Lieutenant-Commander John Hicks, RN
1923–43	Lieutenant-Colonel William Bruce Almon, RCA
1943–49	Mrs. Audrey Dumphy §
1950–64	Mrs. Jean Willetts
1965–70	Mrs. Jean Cole
1971–73	Ms. Marie Murphy
1974–79	Mrs. Sheila Folk
1980–89	Mrs. Sheila K. MacLeod
1989–2000	Mrs. Mary M. McGrath
2000–04	Mrs. Maureen Hope
2005–06	Chief Superintendent William Vye, RCMP
2006–07	Mrs. Barb Reynolds
2007–08	Ms. Julie Stiles ¶
2009–	Dr. Christopher McCreery, MVO

* Previously served as Private Secretary to the Lieutenant Governor of New Brunswick, 1865–67, and later as Secretary to the Governor General of Canada, 1875

** Previously served as Private Secretary to the Lieutenant Governor of New Brunswick, 1869–73

† Rose to rank of Major-General; appointed Companion of the Order of St. Michael and St. George for his service in the First World War

‡ Would go on to become Lieutenant Governor from 1952–58; awarded Military Cross during the First World War and appointed a Queen's Councillor

§ Maiden name was MacDonald, married at Government House in 1944

¶ Surname at time of appointment was Culliton

NOTES

1. James S. Martell, *The Romance of Government House* (Halifax: Queen's Printer, 1965), 24.
2. L.F.S. Upton, "Indian Policy in Colonial Nova Scotia, 1783–1871," *Acadiensis,* vol 5, no. 1, 23.
3. Nova Scotia *Journals of the House of Assembly*, 1874, Appendix no. 8, quoting Order-in-Council of 22 December 1873.
4. *Journals of the House of Assembly*, 9 April, 1888, 129–30.
5. *Halifax Herald*, 22 April 1948.
6. Carolyn A. Young, *The Glory of Ottawa: Canada's First Parliament Buildings* (Montreal: McGill-Queen's University Press, 1995), 62.
7. Colin Read and Donald Forester, "Opera Bouffe: Mackenzie King, Mitch Hepburn, the Appointment of the Lieutenant-Governor and the Closing of Government House Toronto, 1937," *Ontario History*, vol. LXIV, no. 4, 239–40.
8. *British North American*, 21 August 1854.
9. *Journals of the House of Assembly*, 27 March 1855.
10. Sir John Harvey, Lieutenant Governor, opening of the Speech from the Throne, *Journals of the House of Assembly*, 31 January 1856.
11. Brenda Dunn. *A History of Port Royal/Annapolis Royal, 1605–1800* (Halifax: Nimbus Press, 2004), 30.
12. Ibid., 51.
13. Ibid., 118.
14. Charlotte Isabelle Perkins, *The Romance of Annapolis Royal* (Annapolis Royal, 1952), 12–13.
15. Brian C. Cuthbertson, *The Loyalist Governor: Biography of Sir John Wentworth* (Halifax: Petheric Press, 1983), 1.
16. Thomas B. Akins, *History of Halifax City* (Halifax: 1895), 213.
17. Ibid.
18. Ibid.
19. James S. Martell, "Government House," *Bulletin of the Public Archives of Nova Scotia*, vol. 1, no. 4, 1939, 2.
20. Reginald Jeffrey (ed.), *Dyott's Diary, 1781–1841* (London: Archibald Constable & Company, 1907), 36.

21. Sir John Wentworth to Duke of Portland, 25 April 1799, quoted in Martell's "Government House," 4.
22. Akins, 214.
23. Public Archives of Nova Scotia, MG 1 vol. 8, no. 33, *The Infant House in Halifax Burns*.
24. Mary Byers and Margaret McBurney, *Atlantic Hearth* (Toronto: University of Toronto Press, 1994), 14.
25. Hoke P. Kimball and Bruce Henson, *Governor's Houses and State Houses of British Colonial America, 1607–1783; An Historical, Architectural and Archaeological Survey* (Jefferson, North Carolina: McFarlane & Company, 2017), 141.
26. Kimball and Henson, 141.
27. Lawrence Shaw Mayo, *John Wentworth; Governor of New Hampshire, 1767–1775* (Cambridge: Harvard University Press, 1921), 99.
28. Cuthbertson, 8.
29. Mary Beth Noron, *The British-Americans; the Loyalist Exiles in England, 1774–1789* (London: Constable Press, 1974), 49.
30. *London Gazette*, 21 January 1792 (London, 1792), 37.
31. Margaret Ellis, "Governor Wentworth's Patronage," *Nova Scotia Historical Society*, vol. 25, 52.
32. Mayo, 174.
33. Sir Adams George Archibald, "Government House at Halifax," *Report and Collections of the Nova Scotia Historical Society*, 1882–1883, vol. III, 199.
34. Statutes of Province of Nova Scotia, 1799, Chapter IX, 408.
35. In 1797 the Legislature sat from 6 June to 10 July; 1798, 8 June to 7 July; 1799, 7 June to 24 July and 1800, 20 February to 2 May.
36. Government House, Ottawa (Rideau Hall) is 90,000 square feet in floor space.
37. *Journal and proceedings of the House of Assembly of the province of Nova- Scotia, Friday, 7th June, 1799* (Halifax: King's Printer, 1799), 381.
38. Archibald, "Government House at Halifax," 204.
39. D.A. Campbell, *Pioneers of Medicine in Nova Scotia* (Halifax: Maritime Medical News, 1905), 204. Also see, Akins, 69.
40. Sandra Bluntman, "Books of designs for country houses, 1780–1815," *Architectural History*, vol. 11 (1968), 25.
41. Cuthbertson, 109.
42. George Richardson, *A Series of Original Designs for Country Seats* (London, 1795).
43. Thanks is due to Dr. Frances Sands, curator of drawings and books at the Sir John Soane's Museum, London, for her assistance in identifying many of the Adamesque features of Government House Halifax along with the corresponding British buildings that display similar features.
44. Ibid.
45. James S. Martell. The Romance of Government House (Halifax: Queen's Printer, 1965), 13.
46. Ibid.
47. Ibid.
48. Charles Bruce Fergusson, "Isaac Hildrith (c. 1741–1807) Architect of Government House Halifax," *Dalhousie Review*, vol. 50, no. 4, 1971, 515.
49. Sir Adams George Archibald, "Government House at Halifax," *Report and Collections of the Nova Scotia Historical Society*, 1882–1883, vol. III, 204–205.
50. Reply of Sir John Wentworth to the Nova Scotia Legislature, 13 April 1802, quoted in Martell's "Government House," *Bulletin of the Public Archives of Nova Scotia*, vol. 1, no. 4, 1939, 13.
51. Cuthbertson, 108.
52. Garry D. Shutlak, "The history of the Governor's North Farm and Mulgrave Park, Halifax," *The Griffin*, vol. 30., no. 3, September 2005.
53. Chapter 12 of the Acts of 1855, *Second Supplement Containing Ordinances of the City of Halifax N.S., passed in 1854, 1855 and 1856; several Provincial Acts concerning the city, passed in 1855 and 1856* (Halifax: J. & W. Compton, 1856), 34.

54. An Act to Authorize the Board of Works to Lease or Sell Certain Public Property, passed 31 March 1854.
55. Shelagh Mackenzie and Scott Robson, *Halifax Street Names: An Illustrated Guide* (Halifax: Formac Publishing, 2002), 17.
56. The King v Caroll [1948] SCR 126, 130–131.
57. During his decade in office, Archibald refused Royal Assent to six bills and reserved two. J. Murray Beck, *The Government of Nova Scotia* (Toronto: University of Toronto Press, 1957), 183.
58. Since the introduction of the *Interpretation Act*, 1968, it is no longer necessary for holders of Crown offices to swear a new Oath of Allegiance, their loyalty is deemed to automatically transfer to the new Sovereign. It is, however, customary for a proclamation ceremony to be held on the accession of the Sovereign.
59. *Nova Scotia House of Assembly Hansard,* 16 February 1861.
60. *New York Times*, 6 August 1860.
61. Ian Radforth, *Royal Spectacle; the 1860 Visit of the Prince of Wales to Canada and the United States* (Toronto: University of Toronto Press, 2004), 308.
62. Sir Adams George Archibald, "Life of Sir John Wentworth: Governor of Nova Scotia, 1792–1808," *Nova Scotia Historical Society*, vol. 20, 49.
63. Mayo, 174, 181.
64. Royal Archives, GV/PRIV/GVD/1901, diary entry of 19 October 1901.
65. *Evening Mail* 23 June 1911.
66. *Nova Scotian & Weekly Chronicle*, 30 May 1913.
67. The four Governors General who were sworn in at Province House and would stay at Government House were: John Campbell, Marquis of Lorne, sworn in 25 November 1878; Albert Grey, Earl Grey, sworn in 10 December 1904; Victor Cavendish, the Duke of Devonshire, 11 November 1916; and Vere Ponsonby, the Earl of Bessborough, sworn in 4 April 1931.
68. NS Archives MG 20, vol 535, no. 1, Minute Book of the Local Council of Women, August 1894–January 1893, 30 August 1894).
69. Robert Hubbard, *Ample Mansions* (Ottawa: University of Ottawa Press, 1989), 51.
70. Henry James Morgan, *Types of Canadian Women* (Toronto: William Briggs, 1903), 71.
71. *Public Accounts: Province of Nova Scotia*, 1917–18, 348 and *Public Accounts: Province of Nova Scotia*, 1919–20, 274.
72. Janet F. Kitz, *Shattered City: The Halifax Explosion & the Road to Recovery* (Halifax: Nimbus, 2008), 3.
73. Ibid., 58.
74. Ibid., 59.
75. Abraham C. Ratshesky, *Report of the Halifax Relief Expedition, December 6 to 15, 1917* (Boston: Wright and Potter Printing, 1918), 25.
76. Ibid., 25.
77. *Rules & Regulations of the Colonial Service*, 1843, 49.
78. Archibald, 106–7.
79. *Halifax Morning Chronicle*, 2 January 1907.
80. Joseph Pope, *The Tour of Their Royal Highnesses the Duke and Duchess of Cornwall and York, through the Dominion of Canada in the Year 1901* (Ottawa: S.E. Dawson Printer, 1903), 143.
81. *Halifax Herald*, 24 November 1918.
82. *The London Gazette*, No. 30922, 24 September 1918.
83. David MacKeen, *The Order of St. John of Jerusalem in England* (Halifax, 1916). Remarks given at the Order of St. John investiture held in the Ballroom at Government House, 10 May 1916.
84. Ibid.
85. R.L. Kellock, *Report of the Halifax Disorders* (Ottawa: King's Printer, 1945).
86. *Rules & Regulations of the Colonial Service*, 1843, 62.
87. Ibid., 65.

88. *Halifax Herald*, 17 March 1942. Frederick Francis Mathers, who served as lieutenant governor from 1940 to 1942, was unhappy with the state of Government House, which had not had any significant upgrades since the 1901 Royal Tour. It was at Mathers's request that the plumbing was modernized.
89. J. Clarence Webster, *History in a Government House* (Halifax: Nova Scotia Historical Society, 1926). Webster notes of the original plaques: "There are errors in spelling and in dates. Their continuance in such a prominent position is a reflection on the cultural standards of the Province … For the sake of the good name of Nova Scotia, it would seem only right that these tablets should be removed, and replaced." The plaques were installed by G.M. Smith & Co at the cost of $245.00 in advance of the 1901 Royal Tour of the Duke and Duchess of Cornwall and York, *Journals of the Nova Scotia House of Assembly*, 1904, 230.
90. *Journals of the House of Assembly*, 1901, 223.
91. Norman Ward, "The Raising of Pigs By Lieutenant Governors," *Dalhousie Review*, vol. 29, no. 2, 1949, 154.
92. *Nova Scotia House of Assembly Hansard*, 5 April 1880 (Dr. Duncan Campbell).
93. Sir Conrad M. Swan, *Canadian Symbols of Sovereignty* (Toronto: University of Toronto Press, 1977), 123.
94. *Canada Gazette*, 9 February 1974, 471.
95. *The Public Register of Arms, Badges and Flags of Canada*, vol. VI, p. 60.
96. Beck, 183.
97. Brenton Haliburton, *A Colonial Portrait: The Halifax Diaries of Lady Sherbrooke, 1811–1816* (Halifax: Lulu.com, 2012), 87.

BIBLIOGRAPHY

AKINS, Thomas B. *History of Halifax City*. Halifax, 1895.

ARCHIBALD, Sir Adams George. "Government House at Halifax." *Nova Scotia Historical Society*, vol. 3 (1882–83), pp. 197–208.

———. "Life of Sir John Wentworth: Governor of Nova Scotia, 1792–1808, *Nova Scotia Historical Society*, vol. 20 (1921), pp. 43–109.

BECK, J. Murray. *The Government of Nova Scotia*. Toronto: University of Toronto Press, 1957.

BECK, J. Murray. *Joseph Howe*. Montreal: McGill-Queen's University Press, 1981.

BENSEN, William, Wynn BENSEN, Shawna BUTTS, and Robert FINCH. *Duty & Destiny: A Canadian Tribute to Queen Elizabeth II: A remarkable legacy of royal artefacts*. Fredericton: Ampersand Printing, 2015.

BLUTMAN, Sandra. "Books of Designs for Country Houses, 1780–1815." *Architectural History*, vol. 11 (1968), pp. 25–33.

BYERS, Mary, and Margaret MCBURNEY. *Atlantic Hearth: Early Homes and Families of Nova Scotia*. Toronto: University of Toronto Press, 1994.

CAMPBELL, Donald Alexander. *Pioneers of Medicine in Nova Scotia*. Halifax: Maritime Medical News, 1905.

CHISHOLM, Joseph Andrew. *The Speeches and Public Letters of Joseph Howe* (based upon Mr. Annand's edition of 1858). Halifax: The Chronicle Publishing Company Limited, 1909.

COUTTS, Robert (ed.). "Manitoba's Government House at 125." *Manitoba History: The Journal of the Manitoba Historical Society*, no. 58 (June 2008), pp. 29–35.

CUTHBERTSON, Brian C. *The Loyalist Governor: Biography of Sir John Wentworth*. Halifax: Petheric Press, 1983.

Dictionary of Canadian Biography. Toronto: University of Toronto Press.

DOBSON, Henry and Barbara DOBSON. *Heritage Furnishings of Atlantic Canada; A Visual Survey with Pertinent Points*. Kingston: Quarry Press, 2010.

DUNN, Brenda. *A History of Port Royal/Annapolis Royal, 1605–1800*. Halifax: Nimbus Press, 2004.

ELLIS, Margaret. "Governor Wentworth's Patronage." *Nova Scotia Historical Society*, vol. 25 (1942), pp. 43–109.

ELWOOD, Marie. "Government House Today: November 2008." *The Griffin: A Publication of Heritage Trust of Nova Scotia,* vol. 33, no. 4 (December 2008), pp. 15–17.

FERGUSSON, C. Bruce. "Isaac Hildrith (c. 1841–1807) Architect of Government House Halifax." *Dalhousie Review*, vol. 50, no. 4 (1971), pp. 510–16.

———. "Sir Adams G. Archibald." *Nova Scotia Historical Society*, vol. 36 (April 1958).

FORSTER, John. *The Life of Charles Dickens*. London: Chapman & Hall, 1904.

FRANCIS, Mayann. *Mayann Francis: An Honourable Life.* Halifax: Nimbus Press, 2019.

GRANT IRVING, Robert. *Indian Summer; Lutyens, Baker and Imperial Delhi*. New Haven: Yale University Press, 1981.

HALIBURTON, G. Brenton. *A Colonial Portrait: The Halifax Diaries of Lady Sherbrooke, 1811–1816.* Halifax: Lulu.com, 2012.

HARVEY, D.C. "A View of Halifax, 1749–1949." *Proceedings of the Royal Society of Canada*, vol. XLIII, Series III (June 1949), pp. 71–87.

HNATYSHYN, Gerda. *Rideau Hall: Canada's Living Heritage*. Ottawa: Friends of Rideau Hall, 1994.

HRYNIUK, Margaret. *A Tower of Attraction: An Illustrated History of Government House, Regina Saskatchewan.* Winnipeg: Hignell Printing Ltd, 1991.

HUBBARD, Robert H. *Ample Mansions: The Viceregal Residences of the Canadian Provinces*. Ottawa: University of Ottawa Press, 1989.

———. *Rideau Hall: An Illustrated History of Government House, Ottawa*. Ottawa: Queen's Printer, 1967.

KIMBALL, Hoke P., and Bruce HENSON. *Governor's Houses and State Houses of British Colonial America, 1607–1783; An Historical, Architectural and Archaeological Survey.* Jefferson, North Carolina: McFarlane & Company, 2017.

KITZ, Janet F. *Shattered City: The Halifax Explosion & the Road to Recovery*. Halifax: Nimbus Press, 2008.

LE MOINE, J.M. "Castle St. Louis Under the Roses." *The Canadian Magazine of Police, Science Art and Literature,* vol. VI (November 1895–April 1896), pp. 275–81.

MACBEATH, George. *New Brunswick's Old Government House; a pictorial history*. Fredericton: New Ireland Press, 1995.

MACDONALD, James S. "Life and Administration of Governor Charles Lawrence." *Nova Scotia Historical Society*, vol. 12 (1905), pp. 19–58.

MACKENZIE, Shelagh, and Scott ROBSON. *Halifax Street Names: An Illustrated Guide.* Halifax: Formac Publishing, 2002.

MACMILLAN, Margaret, Marjorie HARRIS, and Anna L. DESJARDINS. *Canada's House: Rideau Hall and the Invention of a Canadian Home*. Toronto: Knopf, 2004.

MARTELL, James Stuart. "Government House." *Bulletin of the Public Archives of Nova Scotia*, vol. 1, no. 4 (1939).

———. *The Romance of Government House*. Halifax: Department of Government Services, 1986. (first published in 1939, republished, 1965, 1973, 1979, 1981, 1983, 1986, 1990).

MAYO, Lawrence Shaw. *John Wentworth; Governor of New Hampshire, 1767–1775*. Cambridge: Harvard University Press, 1921.

McAlpines Directories, 1880–1909 various editions.

MORGAN, Henry James. *Types of Canadian Women and of Women who are or have been connected with Canada*. Toronto: William Brigges, 1903.

MURDOCH, Beamish. *A History of Nova Scotia or Acadie.* Halifax: James Barnes, 1867.

NEERING, Rosemary and Tony OWEN. *Government House: The Ceremonial Home of All British Columbians*. Winlaw: Sono Nis Press, 2007.

NORTON, Mary Beth. *The British-Americans; the Loyalist Exiles in England, 1774–1789*. London: Constable Press, 1974.

ORESKO, Robert (ed.). *The Works in Architecture of Robert & James Adam*. London: St. Martin's Press, 1975.

PAUL, Daniel N. *We Were Not the Savages*. Halifax: Fernwood Publishing, 2000.

PAYZANT, John Y. "John William Johnston, first premier of Nova Scotia under responsible government." *Nova Scotia Historical Society*, vol. 16 (1912), pp. 61–92.

POPE, Joseph. *The Tour of Their Royal Highnesses the Duke and Duchess of Cornwall and York, through the Dominion of Canada in the Year 1901*. Ottawa: S.E. Dawson Printer, 1903.

RADFORTH, Ian. *Royal Spectacle: The 1860 Visit of the Prince of Wales to Canada and the United States* Toronto: University of Toronto Press, 2004.

RATSHESKY, Abraham C. *Report of the Halifax Relief Expedition, December 6 to 15, 1917*. Boston: Wright and Potter Printing, 1918.

READ, Colin, and Donald FORESTER. "Opera Bouffe: Mackenzie King, Mitch Hepburn, the Appointment of the Lieutenant-Governor and the Closing of Government House Toronto, 1937," *Ontario History*, vol. LXIV, no. 4 (December 1977), pp. 239–40.

RICHARDSON, George. *A Series of Original Designs for Country Seats*. London, 1795.

ROSS, Jane. *A Vice-Regal Residence; Alberta's Government House*. Edmonton: Government of Alberta, 2013.

Rules and Regulations for Her Majesty's Colonial Service. London: W. Clowes & Sons, 1843.

SHUTLAK, Gary D. "The history of the Governor's North Farm and Mulgrave Park, Halifax." *The Griffin*, vol. 30, no. 3 (September 2005), pp. 1–3.

SUTHERLAND, David. "A Prince, The Governor and Mr. Mayor Halifax and the Politics of Prestige in 1841." *Royal Nova Scotia Historical Society*, vol. 1 (1998), pp. 93–103.

SWAN, Conrad M. *Canada: Symbols of Sovereignty*. Toronto: University of Toronto Press, 1977.

UPTON, Leslie F.S. "Indian Policy in Colonial Nova Scotia." *Acadiensis*, vol. 5, no. 1 (Autumn 1975), pp. 3–31.

VILLENEUVE, René. *Lord Dalhousie: Patron and Collector*. Ottawa: National Gallery of Canada, 2008.

WALLACE, Arthur W. *An Album of Drawings of Early Buildings in Nova Scotia*. Halifax: Nova Scotia Museum, 1976.

WARD, Norman. "The Raising of Pigs By Lieutenant Governors." *Dalhousie Review*, vol. 29, no. 2 (1949), pp. 153–56.

WEBSTER, J. Clarence. *History in a Government House*. Halifax: Nova Scotia Historical Society, 1926.

WILLETT, Edward. *Government House Regina Saskatchewan: An Illustrated History*. Regina: Your Nickle's Worth Publishing, 2016.

YOUNG, Carolyn A. *The Glory of Ottawa: Canada's First Parliament Buildings*. Montreal: McGill-Queen's University Press, 1995.

IMAGE CREDITS

CONTENTS

8, Library and Archives Canada.

FOREWORD

10, Michael Creagen, Photographer.

AUTHOR'S NOTE

12, Communications Nova Scotia, Government of Nova Scotia.

INTRODUCTION

16, Michael Creagen, Photographer; 17, Len Wagg, Communications Nova Scotia, Government of Nova Scotia; 18 (above), Author Photo; 18 (below), Michael Creagen, Photographer; 19, Provincial Archives of Nova Scotia; 20 (above), Michael Creagen, Photographer; 20 (below), Author Collection; 21, Author Photo; 22 (above), Provincial Archives of Nova Scotia; 22 (middle), Michael Creagen, Photographer; 22 (below), Communications Nova Scotia, Government of Nova Scotia; 23 (above), Author Photo; 23 (below), Michael Creagen, Photographer.

ONE

24, Office of the Lieutenant Governor of Manitoba, Government of Manitoba; 25, Communications Nova Scotia, Government of Nova Scotia; 26, Library and Archives Canada; 27, Library and Archives Canada; 28, Provincial Archives of Nova Scotia; 29, Library and Archives Canada; 30 (above), Author Photo; 30 (below), Office of the Governor of New South Wales; 31 (above), Author Collection; 31 (below), *Toronto Star*; 32, Michael Creagen, Photographer; 33 (above), Office of the Lieutenant Governor of Saskatchewan, Government of Saskatchewan; 33 (below), Author Collection.

TWO

34, Library and Archives Canada; 36 (both images), Library and Archives Canada; 37 (above), Provincial Archives of Nova Scotia; 37 (below), Library and Archives Canada; 38, Library and Archives Canada;

39, Provincial Archives of Nova Scotia; 40, Library and Archives Canada; 41, Library and Archives Canada; 42 (above), Smithsonian; 42 (below), Author Collection; 43, Author Collection; 44, Michael Creagen, Photographer; 45, Author Photo; 46 (both images), Author Photo; 48, Office of the Governor of West Bengal, Government of West Bengal (India); 49, Provincial Archives of Nova Scotia.

THREE

50, Government House Halifax Collection; 51, Provincial Archives of Nova Scotia; 52 (above), Nova Scotia Museums; 52 (below left and below right), George Richardson, Photos by Author; 53, Author Collection; 54 (all images), John Elliot Woolford, Art Gallery of Nova Scotia; 55 (all images), ©Sir John Soane's Museum, London. Photography by Ardon Bar Hama; 56 (above), Author Photo; 56 (below), Author Photo; 57, Government House Halifax Collection; 58 (above), Michael Creagen, Photographer; 58 (inset), Provincial Archives of Nova Scotia; 60, Provincial Archives of Nova Scotia; 61, Provincial Archives of Nova Scotia; 63, Michael Creagen, Photographer; 64, Author Photo; 65, Halifax Regional Municipality Archives.

FOUR

66, Michael Creagen, Photographer; 68, Provincial Archives of Nova Scotia; 69, Author Photo; 70 (above), Department of Canadian Heritage; 70 (below), Library and Archives Canada; 71, Provincial Archives of Nova Scotia; 72, Communications Nova Scotia, Government of Nova Scotia; 73 (above), S. Robb, Communications Nova Scotia, Government of Nova Scotia; 73 (below left and below right), Michael Creagen, Photographer; 74 (above), Dalhousie University Archives; 74 (below left), Kelly Clark, Communications Nova Scotia, Government of Nova Scotia; 74 (below right), Library and Archives Canada; 75, Michael Creagen, Photographer; 76 (both images), Michael Creagen, Photographer; 77, Dalhousie University Archives.

FIVE

78, Library and Archives Canada; 80 (above), Royal Collection Trust; 80 (below), Michael Creagen, Photographer; 81, Michael Creagen, Photographer; 82 (left), Michael Creagen, Photographer; 82 (right and below), Provincial Archives of Nova Scotia; 83 (above), Mary Ann Archibald, Artist; 83 (below), Library and Archives Canada; 84 (above), Library and Archives Canada; 84 (middle), Communications Nova Scotia, Government of Nova Scotia; 84 (below), Author Photo; 85, Communications Nova Scotia, Government of Nova Scotia; 86 (above), National Film Board; 86 (below left), Author Photo; 86 (below right), Michael Creagen, Photographer; 87 (above), C. Buckley, Communications Nova Scotia, Government of Nova Scotia; 87 (middle), Michael Creagen, Photographer; 87 (below), S. Robb, Communications Nova Scotia, Government of Nova Scotia; 88, S. Robb, Communications Nova Scotia, Government of Nova Scotia; 89 (above and middle), Office of the Secretary to the Governor General; 89 (below), Michael Creagen, Photographer; 90, Library and Archives Canada; 91 (above), Royal British Columbia Museum; 91 (below), Department of National Defence; 92, Michael Creagen, Photographer; 93 (above), Author Collection; 93 (inset), Author Collection; 94 (above left), Michael Creagen, Photographer; 94 (above right), Communications Nova Scotia, Government of Nova Scotia; 94 (middle left), Author Photo; 94 (middle right), Michael Creagen, Photographer; 94 (below), Communications Nova Scotia, Government of Nova Scotia; 95 (above), Michael Creagen, Photographer; 95 (below), Michael Creagen, Photographer.

SIX

96, Author Collection; 98 (above), Michael Creagen, Photographer; 98 (inset), Provincial Archives of Nova Scotia; 99, Michael Creagen, Photographer; 100, Government House Halifax Collection; 101 (both images), Government House Halifax Collection; 102 (above), Michael Creagen, Photographer; 102 (below), Communications Nova Scotia, Government of Nova Scotia; 103, Government House Halifax Collection; 104 (above), Provincial Archives of Nova Scotia; 104 (below), Michael Creagen, Photographer; 105 (all images), Michael Creagen, Photographer.

SEVEN

106, Michael Creagen, Photographer; 108 (above), Michael Creagen, Photographer; 108 (below), Government House Halifax Collection; 109 (above), Government House Halifax Collection; 109 (below), Communications Nova Scotia, Government of Nova Scotia; 109 (inset), Communications Nova Scotia, Government of Nova Scotia; 110, Provincial Archives of Nova Scotia; 111 (both images), Government House Halifax Collection; 112 (all images), Michael Creagen, Photographer; 113, Michael Creagen, Photographer; 114 (above), Department of National Defence; 114 (below), Provincial Archives of Nova Scotia; 115 (above), Department of National Defence; 115 (middle), Michael Creagen, Photographer; 115 (below), Government House Halifax Collection; 116 (left), Department of National Defence; 116 (right), Michael Creagen, Photographer; 116 (inset), Provincial Archives of Nova Scotia; 117 (above), Author Collection; 117 (below left and below right), Michael Creagen, Photographer; 118 (all images), Michael Creagen, Photographer; 119 (above), Author Photo; 119 (below), Michael Creagen, Photographer; 120 (above left), Michael Creagen, Photographer; 120 (above right), Author Photo; 120 (middle and below), Michael Creagen, Photographer; 121 (above), Library and Archives Canada; 121 (below), Provincial Archives of Nova Scotia.

EIGHT

122, Michael Creagen, Photographer; 124 (all images), Michael Creagen, Photographer; 125, Library and Archives Canada; 126 (left), Michael Creagen, Photographer; 126 (right), Ian McKee; 126 (inset), Brenda Bury, Artist; 127 (both images), Michael Creagen, Photographer; 128 (both images), Michael Creagen, Photographer; 129 (left), Government House Halifax Collection; 129 (right), Library and Archives Canada; 130 (left), Author Photo; 130 (right), Provincial Archives of Nova Scotia; 130 (below), Michael Creagen, Photographer; 131, Library and Archives Canada; 132, Michael Creagen, Photographer; 133 (above and middle), Provincial Archives of Nova Scotia; 133 (below), Government House Halifax Collection; 134 (all images), Michael Creagen, Photographer; 135 (above), Communications Nova Scotia, Government of Nova Scotia; 135 (below), Michael Creagen, Photographer; 136, Provincial Archives of Nova Scotia; 137 (above), Michael Creagen, Photographer; 137 (below), Author Photo; 138, Author Photo; 139, Michael Creagen, Photographer; 140 (above), Communications Nova Scotia, Government of Nova Scotia; 140 (below), Michael Creagen, Photographer; 141 (above), Library and Archives Canada; 141 (below), Nova Scotia Museums; 142 (left), Library and Archives Canada; 142 (right), Government House Halifax Collection; 142 (middle and bottom), Michael Creagen, Photographer; 143, Michael Creagen, Photographer; 144 (above), John Saunders Climo, Photographer; 144 (below), Michael Creagen, Photographer; 145 (above), Library and Archives Canada; 145 (middle), Author Photo; 145 (below), Michael Creagen, Photographer; 146 (all images), Michael Creagen, Photographer; 147 (above and below left), Michael Creagen, Photographer; 147 (below right), Author Photo.

NINE

148, Michael Creagen, Photographer; 150 (above and below right), Michael Creagen, Photographer; 150 (below left), Provincial Archives of Nova Scotia; 151 (above and below), Michael Creagen, Photographer; 151 (middle), Provincial Archives of Nova Scotia; 152, Michael Creagen, Photographer; 153 (all images), Michael Creagen, Photographer; 154 (above), Provincial Archives of Nova Scotia; 154 (below), Michael Creagen, Photographer; 155 (both images), Provincial Archives of Nova Scotia.

TEN

156, Library and Archives Canada; 158 (both images), Michael Creagen, Photographer; 159 (all images), Michael Creagen, Photographer; 160 (above), Michael Creagen, Photographer; 160 (inset above), Author Collection; 160 (inset below), Michael Creagen, Photographer; 161 (above), Provincial Archives of Nova Scotia; 161 (middle and below), Michael Creagen, Photographer; 162, Michael Creagen, Photographer; 163 (above and below), Michael Creagen, Photographer; 163 (inset), Author Collection; 164 (above), Communications Nova Scotia, Government of Nova Scotia; 164 (below), Author Photo; 165, Author Photo; 166 (all images), Library and Archives Canada; 167, Michael Creagen, Photographer; 168 (above), Michael Creagen, Photographer; 168 (below), Provincial Archives of Nova Scotia; 169, Michael Creagen, Photographer.

ELEVEN

170, Michael Creagen, Photographer; 172 (above, top and bottom rows), Michael Creagen, Photographer; 172 (bottom left), Provincial Archives of Nova Scotia; 172 (bottom right), Michael Creagen, Photographer; 173 (above), Robin Watt, Artist; 173 (below), Hedley Graham James Rainnie, Artist; 174 (above and middle), Michael Creagen, Photographer; 174 (below), Office of the Secretary to the Governor General; 175 (above), Brenda Bury, Artist; 175 (below), Provincial Archives of Nova Scotia; 176 (both images), Michael Creagen, Photographer; 177, Michael Creagen, Photographer; 178 (all images), Michael Creagen, Photographer; 179 (above), Alan Syliboy, Artist; 179 (below), Len Wagg, Communications Nova Scotia, Government of Nova Scotia; 180 (both images), Michael Creagen, Photographer; 181 (left), Michael Creagen, Photographer; 181 (right), Mathieu Verlier, Artist; 182 (both images), Michael Creagen, Photographer; 183 (above), Provincial Archives of Nova Scotia; 183 (below), Michael Creagen, Photographer.

TWELVE

184, Author Photo; 186 (left and right), Office of the Secretary to the Governor General; 186 (below), Author Photo; 187, Michael Creagen, Photographer; 188, Office of the Secretary to the Governor General; 189 (above), Communications Nova Scotia, Government of Nova Scotia; 189 (below), Author Photo; 190 (above), Michael Creagen, Photographer; 190 (below), Author Photo; 191 (above), Author Photo; 191 (below), Michael Creagen, Photographer; 192, Michael Creagen, Photographer; 193 (above), Michael Creagen, Photographer; 193 (below), Communications Nova Scotia, Government of Nova Scotia; 195, Office of the Secretary to the Governor General; 196 (both images), Communications Nova Scotia, Government of Nova Scotia; 197 (above), Author Collection; 197 (below), S. Robb, Communications Nova Scotia, Government of Nova Scotia; 198 (left and middle), Author Photo; 198 (right), Michael Creagen, Photographer; 199, Communications Nova Scotia, Government of Nova Scotia; 200, Library and Archives Canada; 201, Michael Creagen, Photographer; 202 (both images), Michael Creagen, Photographer.

INDEX

ABBREVIATIONS AND POST-NOMINALS

AdeC	Honorary Aide-de-Camp
BEM	British Empire Medal
BT	Baronet of the United Kingdom
CB	Companion of the Order of the Bath
CAF	Canadian Armed Forces
CBE	Commander of the Order of the British Empire
CC	Companion of the Order of Canada
CD	Canadian Forces' Decoration
CEF	Canadian Expeditionary Force
CM	Member of the Order of Canada
CMG	Companion of the Order of St. Michael and St. George
CMM	Commander of the Order of Military Merit
DSO	Distinguished Service Order
ED	Efficiency Decoration
GCB	Knight Grand Cross of the Order of the Bath
GCH	Knight Grand Cross of the Royal Guelphic Order
GCMG	Knight Grand Cross of the Order of St. Michael and St. George
GM	George Medal
HMS	Her/His Majesty's Ship
HMCS	Her/His Majesty's Canadian Ship
KC	King's Counsellor
KCB	Knight Commander of the Order of the Bath
KCH	Knight Commander of the Royal Guelphic Order
KCMG	Knight Commander of the Order of St. Michael and St. George
Kt	Knight Bachelor
MC	Military Cross
MD	Medical Doctor
MLA	Member of the Legislative Assembly
MM	Military Medal
MMM	Member of the Order of Military Merit
MP	Member of Parliament
MSM	Meritorious Service Medal
MBE	Member of the Order of the British Empire
MVO	Member of the Royal Victorian Order
OBE	Officer of the Order of the British Empire
OC	Officer of the Order of Canada
OMM	Officer of the Order of Military Merit
ONS	Order of Nova Scotia
PC	Privy Councillor
QC	Queen's Counsellor
RCA	Royal Canadian Academy of Arts Royal Canadian Artillery
RCAF	Royal Canadian Air Force
RCMP	Royal Canadian Mounted Police
RCN	Royal Canadian Navy
RCNVR	Royal Canadian Navy Volunteer Reserve
RN	Royal Navy
RVM	Royal Victorian Medal
SM	Medal of Service of the Order of Canada
VC	Victoria Cross